POLICY & EVIDENCE
IN A PARTISAN AGE

THE GREAT DISCONNECT

Also of interest from the Urban Institute Press:

Contemporary U.S. Tax Policy, second edition,
by C. Eugene Steuerle

War and Taxes, by Steven A. Bank, Kirk J. Stark,
and Joseph J. Thorndike

THE URBAN INSTITUTE PRESS
WASHINGTON, DC

POLICY & EVIDENCE

IN A PARTISAN AGE

THE GREAT DISCONNECT

by Paul Gary Wyckoff

THE URBAN INSTITUTE PRESS
2100 M Street, N.W.
Washington, D.C. 20037

Library of Congress Cataloging-in-Publication Data

Wyckoff, Paul Gary.
    Policy and evidence in a partisan age: the great disconnect / Paul Gary Wyckoff.
        p. cm.
    Includes bibliographical references and index.
    ISBN 978-0-87766-749-0 (pbk.: alk. paper)
    1. Political planning—United States—History—21st century. 2. Political parties—United States—History—21st century. 3. United States—Politics and government—2001- I. Title.
    JK468.P64W95 2009
    320.60973—dc22

                                                                                2008056021

Printed in the United States of America

13 12 11 10 09   1 2 3 4 5

#297146549

THE URBAN INSTITUTE is a nonprofit, nonpartisan policy research and educational organization established in Washington, D.C., in 1968. Its staff investigates the social, economic, and governance problems confronting the nation and evaluates the public and private means to alleviate them. The Institute disseminates its research findings through publications, its web site, the media, seminars, and forums.

Through work that ranges from broad conceptual studies to administrative and technical assistance, Institute researchers contribute to the stock of knowledge available to guide decisionmaking in the public interest.

Conclusions or opinions expressed in Institute publications are those of the authors and do not necessarily reflect the views of officers or trustees of the Institute, advisory groups, or any organizations that provide financial support to the Institute.

Contents

Acknowledgments

Early versions of parts of this book were presented at seminars at Hamilton College and Union College, and I received numerous helpful comments and suggestions. I am indebted to Therese McCarty of Union College for reading early chapters and giving useful and encouraging feedback. Two anonymous reviewers provided lots of constructive criticism and suggestions. I would like to thank Devlan O'Connor for her patient, thorough editing, which resulted in a tighter, easier-to-read manuscript. And, as always, I am enormously grateful to my wife, April, whose continuing faith sustains me.

1

Introduction
The Oversold Society

Democracy is a method of finding proximate solutions to insoluble problems.
—Reinhold Niebuhr

Leave your theory, as Joseph his coat in the hands of the harlot, and flee.
—Ralph Waldo Emerson

Today we take it as a given that the state of the economy affects presidential elections. Ronald Reagan won the 1980 election after he stared into the camera during a debate with Jimmy Carter and asked the voters whether they were better off than four years ago. Bill Clinton won the 1992 election by keeping his campaign focused on "the economy, stupid." And most recently, Barack Obama's November 2008 victory over George Bush was certainly aided by the long recession that began in December of 2007.

Since 1960, the American National Election Studies have surveyed voters about the most important problem facing the nation. From 1960 to 2000, the most common answer was a concern about the economy or business or consumer issues, easily outpacing foreign policy or national defense issues (Johnston and Williamson 2005). Among academics, a small industry has formed to assess the effect of economic conditions on voting; by 2006, the number of scholarly articles and books stood at 400 (Lewis-Beck and Stegmaier 2007). The articles have found that economic conditions have strong and statistically significant impacts on how people vote. The best known of these pieces are by economist Ray Fair of Yale University; in a 1996 article, Fair was able to explain 96 percent of the variation in the votes for president from 1916 to 1992 by looking only at growth rates, inflation rates, whether an incumbent was running again, and whether the country was at war.

For Barack Obama, the same recession that swept him into power came to dominate every other issue in his administration. Ambitious plans on health care and energy played second fiddle to fiscal stimulus bills and decisions about bailing out investment firms. In an interview shortly after his inauguration Obama admitted, "Look, the only measure of my success as president when people look back five years from now or nine years from now is going to be, did I get this economy fixed? . . . I'm not going to be judged on whether or not I got a pet project here or there, I'm going to be judged on, have we pulled ourselves out of recession?"[1]

But are the voters' expectations rational in this regard? As a practical matter, what can the president really do about the economy? A review of the evidence shows that there is an enormous gap between the public's *perception* of the president as an economic catalyst and the *reality* of the president's power in this area. Indeed, the evidence suggests that voters pondering their decisions ought to ignore President Reagan's question about their economic circumstances.

Among prominent macroeconomists, many believe that fiscal policy cannot have real effects on the economy because of something called the Ricardian equivalence theorem. The consensus among the remaining macroeconomists is that, although fiscal policy can theoretically boost the economy, the time needed to recognize business cycles and the long lags involved in implementing policy make it extremely difficult for presidential administrations to have positive impacts on the economy (see chapter 3). An analysis by William Keech (1995, 162) of postwar economic stimulus packages before 1995 showed that *all* of them took effect too late to help aid economic recovery: "There is no example of a program that was passed before the final month of the recession it was designed to correct." In a review of fiscal policy over the last 40 years, Bradford DeLong (1996, 47) concluded, "Looking back at the budget since World War II, it is difficult to argue that on balance 'discretionary' fiscal policy has played *any* stabilizing role" (italics from the original).

As discussed in chapter 3, even the New Deal programs of the 1930s had little effect on recovery from an economic downturn. The Great Depression was so long that it gave policymakers plenty of time to rec-ognize the problem and craft innovative responses. And the sweeping mandate given to Franklin Roosevelt in the 1932 and 1936 elections gave him free reign to run unprecedented peacetime deficits. Yet among eco-nomic historians, there is widespread consensus that FDR's fiscal poli-cies were not a major factor in bringing us out of the Depression.

It seems likely, then, that we elect presidents to perform a task over which they have little control, and we pay insufficient attention to the things they can do, such as conducting foreign policy and ensuring that the federal government efficiently provides public services. Voting your wallet for a presidential election is a bit like choosing a news broadcast depending upon whether the news was good or bad the last time you tuned in to that station. The news would have been just as good (or just as bad) regardless of who was behind the anchor desk.

However, this contrast between the claims of public debate and the reality of government power is not unique to the presidency or to national economic issues. While debates on education tend to center on testing, class size, and teacher qualifications, the disappointing conclusion reached by education studies is that the effects of public schooling are dwarfed by the influences of family and socioeconomic background. And while gubernatorial campaigns center on attracting new jobs and stimulating the economy, the literature suggests that state tax and spending policies have little effect. Similarly, while welfare policies focus on altering the educational, marriage, divorce, and childbearing decisions of the poor, there is surprisingly little evidence that we can do so.

The purpose of this book is to explore this paradox between the exaggerated claims made for public policy interventions and the reality of their limited effectiveness. Because policy impacts are often overstated, our national debate is misguided, concentrating on illusory "fixes" rather than on the true choices before us. I provide detailed examples of such overstatements in five areas: short-term fiscal policy, long-term growth policy, education, state and local economic development, and welfare. Each of my arguments is grounded in the best available evidence—literature reviews of the quantitative empirical work in each field. The book analyzes the reasons for this paradox, and makes recommendations for changes in the way we teach economics, statistics, and law in order to narrow the gap between rhetoric and reality. The following chapters emphasize three themes, which are briefly summarized in the sections below.

Disconnected Levers

Government policy is consistently oversold, to citizens, to politicians, and even to academics. It is oversold by both conservatives and liberals, in different but curiously similar ways. Over and over, we elect officials in the naïve belief that they can pull some magic lever to fix our social and economic problems. When that doesn't work, we "throw the bums out" and elect someone else to pull a different lever or to pull the same lever in the opposite direction. But what many Americans don't understand, but empirical studies bear out, is that in many circumstances the governmental levers are simply disconnected from the problems they are supposed to address.

The Three Views of Government Policy

The first view of policy, the liberal view, is that government policy can change the world, that it can fundamentally alter the social, economic, and demographic fabric of our society. After a decade of teaching courses on the application of statistics to public policy and having reviewed countless empirical articles on the effects of government programs, my conclusion is that it typically does not. The record shows remarkably little evidence that government programs can alter these fundamental factors. The growth of the service economy, the decline of traditional family structures, the acceleration of globalization, the appearance of new technologies that both threaten established industries and change how we interact—all of these inexorable changes are, I would argue, largely beyond our control.

Since Ronald Reagan, conservatives have done an excellent job of pointing out holes in this first view. But what is less well recognized is that conservatives suffer from a parallel fallacy. The second view of the world, the conservative view, is that government policy is not the *remedy* for social problems but is actually the *cause* of those problems. As Reagan put it in his first inaugural address in 1981, "Government is not the solution, it's the problem." Permissive welfare policies, so the theory goes, encourage families to break up, encourage parents to have more children, and encourage workers to quit their jobs and take government assistance (see chapter 9). High taxes, conservatives argue, drive industries out of the city, the state, and the country, leading to unemployment and slow growth (see chapters 4 and 7). The irony here is that conservatives see government as powerful, just as liberals do, but with opposite effects. Many of these fundamental social problems could be solved, according to conservatives, if we just got the government out of the way.

Again, the empirical literature on the effects of government programs and taxes indicates that, in most cases, conservatives greatly oversell the power of government actions. A look at the data suggests that our economy and our society are being shaped by powerful historical forces that are largely independent of government policy. Welfare programs probably have little to do with the increase in out-of-wedlock births, and tax policies have little to do with the distribution of economic growth or the ebb and flow of economic activity over time.

Throughout this book, I argue for a third view of government policy, based on the empirical literature—one that acknowledges the limitations of government policy for good and for ill. This third view concentrates on what we *can* control about policy problems, rather than on what we *cannot* control. If government cannot solve the fundamental problem of poverty in a capitalist economy, it can have a profound effect in relieving suffering and ameliorating hardships among the poor. If public policy cannot alter the fundamental forces of globalization and post-industrialization, it can nevertheless help people adapt to these changes and reduce the pain and suffering they cause. Rather than chasing after imaginary solutions to social problems, the third view focuses on helping people cope with them.

The Elements of Government Programs

Domestic government programs contain various levels of five fundamental activities: redistributional, investment, service, regulatory, and behavioral. A *redistributional* activity is one that simply moves money from one group of citizens to another. Social Security remains our most popular federal program precisely because it doesn't try to do anything beyond giving money to old and disabled citizens. It doesn't try to convince senior citizens to work more, or stay married, or go back to school. Since it is not measured by such yardsticks, Social Security is considered successful by the only yardstick left: whether it has raised the incomes of senior citizens and disabled people, bringing them out of poverty.

An *investment* activity is one that directs money into human or physical capital in the expectation of greater productivity in the future. The federal highway system or federally sponsored basic medical research, for example, are highly investment-oriented programs.

A *service* activity is one that provides citizens with goods or services. For example, a lighthouse provides an invaluable service to mariners at sea, and an airport control tower provides essential services for airplane pilots and passengers.

A *regulatory* activity is one that establishes rules for social and economic activity. The federal courts enforce property rights, for example. Antitrust regulations prohibit monopolies, antipollution legislation restricts individuals and companies from damaging the environment, and work-place safety requirements ensure that firms do not abuse their workforces.

My focus in this book is on the fifth element of government programs—the *behavioral* component. Behavioral activities try to change targeted groups' behavior, such as reducing teenage pregnancy, or convincing a company to change the location of a plant, or getting children to read more. Although the behavioral element is only one of five elements, it receives a disproportionate share of our attention in public debates. Typically, political discussion of the national economy is all about getting consumers to spend more or getting firms to invest more. Talk of local economic development centers on getting firms to move to a particular state or locality. Debates on welfare always seem to return to the question of getting welfare recipients to work more, marry more, and have fewer babies.

Notice that many controversial programs are actually a combination of these five components. What we call welfare is a combination of a redistributive element (cash and services) and a behavioral element (provisions to get the poor to stay married, have fewer children, and have children later). And what we call education is a combination of an investment element (increasing human capital), a service element (providing learning experiences for children), and a behavioral element (getting children to learn more and pursue higher education). The lines between redistributive, investment, service, regulatory, and behavioral elements of programs are often blurry. Nevertheless, my thesis is that, despite the claims of conservatives and liberals, the behavioral impact of domestic public policy in the United States is usually small in relation to that of other social forces at work.[2] This means that we really ought to be evaluating government programs by focusing on the other four elements of policy, rather than concentrating on the behavioral element so often discussed by politicians and the news media. Not all redistributional, investment, service, or regulatory activities are successful, of course—money can be wasted in administration, or wrongly invested, or used to provide services people don't want. My point is simply that we ought to judge our leaders based on their demonstrated performance in those four areas, rather than on an illusory ability to change behavior.

An Illustration of the Pattern

The theoretical overestimation of public policies is vividly illustrated in the issue of public financing for sports stadiums. Given its finite resources, a community faces a choice between sports services and other things it might do with its money. Suppose that the community is approached by a sports team or a group of investors about building a sports stadium. Under the first view of government policy,[3] the public discussion about the stadium will be all about theoretical economic benefits: more construction jobs, increased tourism, new jobs at the ballpark, and growth in the restaurant and hotel businesses. The argument will be that the new park will be an expenditure that pays for itself in faster economic growth and new tax revenues.

The second view of government policy is skeptical of the government's ability to recognize profitable growth opportunities and its ability to seize on them. The construction jobs are temporary, and much of the spending at the ballpark will simply divert expenditures from other local entertainment. The jobs at the ballpark are often part-time, low-wage service positions, and much of the profit goes to owners and highly paid athletes who live elsewhere. Under the second view, government subsidization of sports stadiums actually makes the local economic situation worse by wasting precious local capital. If the local government raises taxes to support the new ballpark, the new taxes will weaken the incentives to invest in the city, reducing jobs and economic growth. As in the first view, the policy debate centers strictly on the economic factors of job growth, income increases, and multiplier effects.

But a look at the empirical literature on sports stadiums reveals weaknesses in both the first and second views of public policy. These studies show a strong consensus that sports stadiums are not major engines of economic growth. By themselves, stadiums cannot turn around the fortunes of inner cities, and they cannot pay for themselves in the long run with increased tax revenues (Noll and Zimbalist 1997, 15). These findings call into question the first view of ballpark economics. What stadiums do provide, however, is more entertainment and sports services, because they hold the key to the location of sports franchises. New clubs will typically refuse to locate in an area without an attractive new stadium, and older clubs threaten to move unless provided with up-to-date facilities. Sports teams do unite communities: in increased community pride, in a sense of shared experience. Using survey data, scholars have been able to demonstrate the intangible benefits of sports franchises, and these may be large enough to justify public investment (Rappaport and Wilkerson 2001). These findings suggest that the first and second views, with their tight focus on economic factors, may ignore crucial community benefits.

Is building the stadium with public assistance a good idea? Once we abandon liberals' and conservatives' theoretical arguments and simply rely on the highest-quality empirical information available, a different perspective emerges. The lesson of the third view of public policy is this: forget the inflated estimates of job growth and dubious spending multipliers. And forget the exaggerated talk about tax disincentives—as chapter 7 will demonstrate, state and local tax rates have small impacts on economic activity. The real question is whether the community is willing to pay the freight for the personal and psychological benefits of having a team in town. The authors of the largest and most comprehensive study of the economics of sports stadiums put it this way: "Properly reckoned, the value of a sports team to a city should not be measured in dollars of new income but should be appreciated as a potential source of entertainment and civic pride that comes with a substantial net cost" (Noll and Zimbalist 1997, 498).

In terms of the five-part division of government activities discussed above, the first and second views of policy have been looking at the wrong element entirely. These have been concentrating on the behavioral element of sports stadiums—how they can change the behavior of fans and firms and improve local economic conditions. But that's an illusion—the behavioral effects are much smaller than we thought. Instead, we should look at the service element of the question. Sports franchises provide a service to their communities—a place for recreation and a common bond between citizens. The right question to ask here is not "how will this stadium change our town?" but rather "are the benefits of this franchise worth the costs to our citizens?"

Explanations from Political Science and Psychology

Political scientists would probably be unsurprised by our first theme. Of course politicians overstate the effects of their policies; they have every incentive to do so if distorting information will enhance their careers. Voters are "rationally ignorant"—their share of the costs or benefits of any particular program is too small to warrant careful analysis of politicians' claims. In addition, voters are not always rational deliberators of policy options; as Kathleen Hall Jamieson puts it (1992, 41), "our quirks as consumers of political information" make us particularly susceptible to negative information, cause us to pay disproportionate attention to vivid case studies, diminish our reasoning capacity in fearful situations, and make us believe that repeated messages are more credible. According to political scientists, the problem is not so much a lack of information, but a distorted political system that allows policymakers (or, as political scientists call them, policy elites) to dupe irrational voters into making poor choices.

The trouble with the political science perspective is that it assumes politicians know the truth and deliberately mislead the rest of us. But the evidence suggests otherwise. As detailed in chapter 8, politicians' educational backgrounds are strong in economic theory and legal procedure, but terribly weak in statistics and empirical policy studies. For example, an examination of the curricula of six of the top law schools in the country revealed that none of them required a course in statistics, and only 3 percent of the students took advantage of optional statistics courses that were offered at three of the schools.[4] Chapter 5 details the poor quality of the information used in making policy decisions by contrasting it with the data and analysis used in medical decisions. For example, the evidence underlying the largest tax cut in U.S. history consisted of a weak analogy to a tax cut during the Kennedy administration. Taken together, these chapters demonstrate that elites are not omniscient Machiavellians, but suffer from the same misinformation and confusion as the rest of us. Certainly politics and political gamesmanship play a role in poor decisions, but learning to understand and interpret the evidence is a vital prerequisite to making better choices.

Psychologists would probably also be unsurprised that policy levers are disconnected. In 1975, Ellen J. Langer showed that people systematically overestimate their control over circumstances, a result she called "the illusion of control." In one experiment, Langer's subjects strongly preferred a lottery ticket they chose over one another person chose, even if both tickets had an equal probability of winning. Some research even indicates that the illusion of control is beneficial in some circumstances because it leads to greater optimism and perseverance. Alloy and Clements (1992) showed that college students with stronger illusions of control were less discouraged by poor test results and negative life experiences than more realistic students. Of course we overestimate our abilities—that is one means of coping with an uncertain and unyielding world.

My point in this book is not to dispute political scientists and psychologists, but to find ways around the problems they raise. Ultimately, our political beliefs are dysfunctional, and given the magnitude of the issues facing us, we simply cannot afford to let them stand unchallenged. For example, real human lives are involved in the welfare debate—mostly children's. Getting welfare policy wrong means subjecting those children to real suffering, including hunger, isolation, illness, and poor life prospects. Can we really afford to remain ignorant about the problem or react to information irrationally?

Unfortunately, the political science and psychological explanations for disconnected levers aren't helpful in solving the problem. Knowing that politicians sometimes distort the facts doesn't help much, because we need to know exactly how the facts are distorted in order to clarify our understanding. Knowing that we are subject to illusions of control isn't helpful, unless we know which areas are subject to illusion and how far our illusions stray from reality. What we really need are some empirical observations about when we are typically fooled and some benchmarks against which to measure both politicians' claims and our beliefs about the world.

The next two themes, therefore, deal with identifying the circumstances in which we overstate policy outcomes and with educating us—and our policymakers—to think clearly about policy issues.

Too Much Theory, Not Enough Values

The ideological overestimation of government policy is aided by a parallel *theoretical* overestimation. Due to the power, precision, and sophistication of economic tools, particularly theoretical ones, policymakers tend to clothe their arguments in economic theory. Since labor supply curves slope up, the argument goes, a tax on wages reduces the net wage and reduces the supply of labor, increasing unemployment. A worker-training program, it seems, increases the marginal productivity of labor, increasing wages and employment. And universal health insurance ought to decrease the welfare rolls, since the current system penalizes mothers who try to give up welfare (which provides health insurance) for low-wage work (which often does not).

All of this makes perfect sense in the two-dimensional, static world of undergraduate economics courses. The trouble is that, although everyone knows that demand curves slope down and supply curves slope up, only a very few have the education and motivation to estimate the slopes of the curves, and these parameters have a profound effect on the practicality of policy prescriptions. Since we approach policy problems from a theoretical, rather than empirical, standpoint, we fail to appreciate that in the complex, multidimensional world in which we live, the individual effects of government policies are often small.

In the case of welfare policy, for instance, economic theory suggests that higher welfare benefits encourage welfare mothers to have more children, because increasing the marginal benefits of any activity ought to get us to do more of that activity. But the childbearing decision is extremely complex, involving availability of birth control, education, class, family structure, and race. When most analysts have looked at the numbers on birth rates and welfare mothers, they have concluded that welfare benefits have almost no effect on birth rates; government policy is a piccolo in a veritable symphony of causes (chapter 9).

Because the language of economics is powerful, we use it to oversell the positive or negative effects of government policies, arguing for increases or reductions in government activity. Once we abandon the inflated expectations of government policy embodied in the first and second views, preferences matter a great deal more than is generally acknowledged. Economists give these preferences an abstract name like "the social welfare function," but political scientists and philosophers use terms like "values" and "ethical judgments."

Politicians continually try to skirt the knotty questions of values by resorting to theoretical, economic arguments, but the empirical evidence draws us right back into the normative sphere. The question is not what welfare system will fix the problem of poverty—none currently available will do that (see chapter 9)—but what welfare system is compatible with our obligations toward the poor (whatever those may be). The question is not what economic development policy will revitalize our state's economy—no such policies currently exist (see chapter 7)—but what economic development policy will help us build a community that matches our preferences. The question is not what fiscal policy will eliminate the swings of the business cycle—at present, we don't have the tools to do these things (see chapter 3)—but what tax policy represents a fair sharing of the public-service burden.

Statistical Innumeracy

The book's final theme concerns the widespread inability of citizens and policymakers to understand basic statistical concepts. In chapter 5, I attempt to illustrate the empirical poverty of our policy debates by contrasting them with debates in health care. In 1981, two landmark decisions were made within weeks of each other. In July, the medical community approved a controversial vaccine for hepatitis B; in August, the Reagan administration engineered the largest tax cut in the history of the country. The claims for the hepatitis vaccine were backed by one of the most successful experimental trials in U.S. history; the claims for the tax cut had almost no empirical support.

If politicians "sell" us distorted information, why are we willing to "buy" it? Why are our standards for evidence in policy disputes so low? Part of the answer may lie in the public's lack of statistical knowledge. Because we don't know how to weigh empirical evidence, we fall victim to poorly supported but intuitively plausible ideas. This lack of sophistication is fed by unhelpful teaching approaches in three disciplines.

In *economics,* the primary emphasis is on learning the theoretical mechanics of demand, supply, and markets, not on the empirical magnitudes of economic phenomena. In fact, nonmajors who take an economics class rarely receive any instruction at all in statistics or econometrics. This leaves them with a head full of theoretical pathways by which government policy could conceivably affect market outcomes, but with no means to discern which actions are most likely to work.

In *statistics,* our current approach emphasizes theoretical concepts (such as probability theory) rather than the application of those concepts to real problems. And when statistical theories are applied to real problems, they are most often focused on experimental statistics in health care, not on the nonexperimental statistics common to public policy.

In *law,* the background favored by the vast majority of politicians, almost no time is devoted to the study of statistics. While students are extremely well trained in the legal nuances of particular cases and in learning to distinguish the fine details between cases, they have almost no training in making valid inferences from a large body of such cases. District attorneys, for example, are well prepared to prosecute and convict as many defendants as possible; but if elected to the town council or the mayor's office, they are not prepared to decide how to allocate scarce resources to best control crime.

The examples in this book do not show that government policy never affects behavior—only that these effects are typically overstated. For example, in the cases of education and state economic development discussed in chapters 6 and 7, policy has a positive effect but one that is much smaller than commonly assumed. To make sensible policy, decision-makers and their advisers must have a realistic appreciation of the relevant parameters and the inevitable policy trade-offs. Such an appreciation requires the ability to draw valid conclusions from masses of data, which is precisely what inferential statistics teaches us.

To see the policy world clearly, we do not have to turn students into printout-carrying statistical geeks. They simply must learn the skills to be knowledgeable consumers of statistical information. Paying attention to the appropriate evidence, I will argue, typically leads us toward the third view of public policy.

Organization of the Book

These three themes—disconnected levers, overreliance on economic theory, and statistical innumeracy—are woven together in the remaining chapters of this book. Chapter 2 explains the empirical methodology we can use to sort out effective from ineffective policies. For those tempted to skip this chapter, let me add a word of encouragement here. I promise: no Greek letters, no equations, and a minimum of multisyllabic technical terms. My goal is to explain the differences in quality of statistical evidence in straightforward, nonmathematical terms. I do so early in the book, so that you can appreciate the strength (and often, weakness) of the evidence debated in the rest of the book. Think of our political discourse as a flea market for policy ideas—it helps to know some indicators of quality beforehand. Chapter 2 provides some things to look for before you "buy" a particular policy prescription.

Chapters 3, 4, 6, 7, and 9 explore five policy areas that illustrate the oversold policy pattern. These chapters address the first two themes of the book. The cases were not randomly selected but do represent voters' most frequently cited domestic concerns. As discussed above, the American National Election Studies[5] show that the most frequently cited domestic problem was a concern about economic conditions (including business and consumer issues). The next most commonly mentioned problem was social welfare (including public welfare and education).[6] Accordingly, the book contains multiple cases from each category.

Chapter 3 examines federal fiscal policy, particularly the role of the president and Congress in the short-term behavior of the economy. Chapter 4 explores the connections between government policy and economic growth. And chapter 7 takes up the issue of state economic development, specifically the tax incentives used in bidding wars between states for jobs. Chapter 6 addresses education policy, focusing on the effect of increased educational resources on student performance. Finally, chapter 9 discusses welfare policy, which has been transformed by the 1996 welfare reform act.

Chapters 5, 8, and 10 illustrate the final theme of statistical innumeracy. As mentioned above, chapter 5 illustrates the current low standards for empirical support currently used by policymakers, by contrasting the evidence medical professionals use to make decisions with the evidence policymakers use. Chapter 8 explores the role of statistics in current economics and legal education. In chapter 10, I make recommendations for changing the way we teach economics, law, and statistics, so that we will be less vulnerable to overzealous claims about the effects of public policies. Because statistical innumeracy is so entwined with the other two themes of the book, chapters 5, 8, and 10 are interspersed with the five chapters examining substantive policy areas.

Too often, our national debates are misguided. We debate phantoms and mirages while leaving the real choices undiscussed. We can only make effective decisions if we are clear about the things that we can, and cannot, change. I hope this book contributes to a better understanding of the true alternatives in front of us.

2

How to Tell What the Emperor Is Wearing

Standards for Evidence in Policy Debates

In Hans Christian Anderson's famous tale "The Emperor's New Clothes," two con men convince the emperor that they have made him an exquisite new suit, but one stupid people cannot see. Of course, the suit does not exist, but everyone convinces themselves that the suit is real. This collective illusion is reinforced by the behavior of everyone around them. Finally, the emperor wears his new "suit" in a magnificent procession, and everyone pretends to admire it, until a little boy blurts out that the emperor has nothing on. His father realizes that the boy is right and says so, which causes other people to admit the truth, until at last the whole crowd cries out, "But he has nothing on at all!"

In some ways, we are like the crowd around the emperor: are we seeing clearly, or is our vision clouded by our preconceptions, our expectations of what we "should" see? Evidence is the only means of escape from these self-delusions. Do welfare benefits encourage poor women to have more children? Do they encourage these women to leave their husbands and boyfriends? Do the benefits discourage marriage? To weigh the evidence on both sides of policy questions like these and to understand the limits of knowledge on the effects of policy, you must have some idea about what separates good evidence from bad evidence. In this chapter, I explain the basis for the evidentiary judgments used in the chapters that follow, showing you how to tell what the emperor is (or is not) wearing.

I illustrate the basic concepts with examples that concentrate on the effects of welfare on family structure.

Parsing the Data: Sampling Error and Confounding Factors

Politicians make claims all the time about the effects of past policies and the likely effects of proposed policies. And they frequently present evidence to bolster their claims. Does the evidence justify the claims? The quality of the evidence presented can be judged by its ability to overcome two great statistical problems: sampling error and confounding factors.

Policy questions are fundamentally questions about human behavior, and human behavior is fiendishly complex. Because huge numbers of causal factors are involved, behavioral responses vary both *across individuals* and *across circumstances for one individual.* Hence, generalizations about behavior must deal with both kinds of variability.

Consider a woman's decision whether to have a baby—a complex decision involving an enormous number of factors, including the woman's economic, health, and marital statuses; her religious beliefs; and her plans for the future. These factors vary across both individuals and circumstances. A low-income woman might make a different decision than a wealthy woman, and the same woman might make a different decision as a teenager than she would make in her mid-thirties.

Sampling error occurs when we generalize from one person or a group of people that is uncharacteristic of the entire population. If the government sought to examine the effect of welfare on birth rates, it would be inaccurate to survey only African American welfare recipients, or Roman Catholic welfare recipients, or Hispanic welfare recipients, or recipients over the age of 40. The results from such a survey could not be generalized to make conclusions about the overall effect of welfare on fertility rates. Even if we were to survey a random sample of all welfare recipients, there is always a chance that the particular sample could be unusual in some way and doesn't represent the welfare population as a whole. But in general, random samples minimize sampling error better than nonrandom samples do, and large samples are better than small samples. The larger the sample, the lower the possibility of it being peculiar in some way.

Short of surveying an entire population (which is usually either extremely expensive or impractical), there is no way to eliminate sampling error. But remarkably, statisticians have developed ways to better cope with it by estimating the likelihood that a particular result could occur just by chance, even if the salient policy variable has no effect on the social problem of interest. This likelihood is then used as a benchmark to gauge the quality of a statistical result.

For example, suppose we are studying the effect of day care services on the work behavior of welfare recipients, and that a sample of 10 shows that providing day care does increase the probability that a welfare recipient will work. Analysts might be tempted to conclude immediately that day care is an effective way to get welfare recipients working, but sampling error stands in their way. What if the sample were unusual, and we just happened to select 10 women who have a strong personal desire to work, independent of day care? By calculating the odds that a particular result is due to chance, scientists make judgments about the effectiveness of policies. If a particular result is likely to have occurred by chance, it is dismissed as "statistically insignificant" and the policy variable involved (in this case, day care) is considered ineffective, even if it did work in this particular study. If the result is unlikely to have occurred by chance, then the results are said to be "statistically significant" and day care is accepted as an effective factor in work behavior.

Confounding factors occur whenever the apparent relationship between one factor and another (say, welfare benefits and birth rates) is muddied by the presence of other relevant factors. Explicitly or implicitly, policy debates are usually about some causal relationship—the effect of policy tool A on social problem B. If, for example, divorce rates are higher among welfare recipients in California than among welfare recipients in Alabama, can this be attributed to higher welfare benefits in California? Not without further examination, because incomes are generally higher in California, and previous empirical studies suggest that higher incomes are associated with higher divorce rates, presumably because unhappy couples have the financial means to set up separate households. Other confounding factors include the states' different religious, cultural, and ethnic make-up. Just as static in a radio transmission makes understanding and appreciating a radio program more difficult, these intervening factors make it more difficult for the analyst to understand and appreciate the true relationship between welfare and fertility decisions.

A Hierarchy for Policy Evidence

The quality of each kind of statistical evidence can be assessed by its vulnerability to the empirical pathologies just described. Figure 2.1 presents a simple hierarchy for empirical evidence.[1]

Case Studies and Anecdotes

> There's a woman in Chicago. She has 80 names, 30 addresses, 12 Social Security cards and is collecting veterans benefits on four nonexisting deceased husbands. And she's collecting Social Security on her cards. She's got Medicaid, getting food stamps and she is collecting welfare under each of her names. Her tax-free cash income alone is over $150,000.
>
> Ronald Reagan, campaigning for the Republican presidential nomination in Gilford, New Hampshire, as quoted in the *New York Times*, February 15, 1976.

Figure 2.1. A Hierarchy of Statistical Information

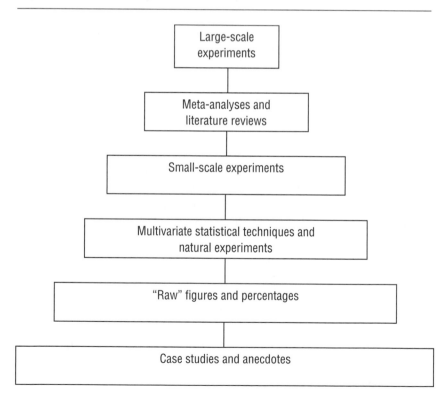

At the bottom of the empirical food chain are simple anecdotes and case studies. On an emotional and persuasive level, such stories can be hugely effective—there is something about a simple, vivid case that sticks in our minds. But on a rational level, simple anecdotes are riddled with holes from sampling error. With such a small sample size, there is a great possibility that the case, however memorable, may be unrepresentative of the population at large.

After candidate Reagan gave the anecdote above, he faced a lot of questions from the press as they tried to verify the existence of "the woman in Chicago" and document the abuses of the welfare system. But even if the story were true, the more important question would be whether this woman is typical of welfare recipients or is an aberration. Of course welfare fraud is immoral, but should we make general welfare policy, affecting all welfare recipients, based on one extreme case?

"Raw" Figures and Percentages

We have the longest peacetime expansion in history, nearly 19 million new jobs; the lowest unemployment in a generation; the lowest minority unemployment ever recorded; the highest home ownership in history. From a deficit of $290 billion, we are moving to a surplus of $99 billion. And this year alone we will pay $85 billion on our national debt.

And a big part of this is the decision the American people, through their elected Representatives, made to end welfare as we know it. We raised the minimum wage and passed the earned-income tax credit, which says to working families: If you work full-time, you shouldn't have to raise your children in poverty. We gave 43 waivers to States to launch their own welfare reform efforts when I took office. And then in 1996, as has already been said, a big bipartisan majority, big majorities of both parties and both Houses reached across the divide to pass this welfare reform bill.
President Bill Clinton, remarks at the National Forum
on Welfare to Work, August 3, 1999.

Next in the hierarchy in figure 2.1 are "raw" figures and percentages. By "raw" figures, I mean figures without context—for example, figures for the United States as a whole. By percentages, I mean similar figures with a context—for example, the percentage of women on welfare who live in the inner city. Often, the additional perspective provided by percentage figures makes them more useful for understanding the problem at hand. But both kinds of figures are subject to enormous problems with confounding factors. Raw figures and percentages by themselves cannot separate the various factors that affect some social outcome: they reflect the total effect of these factors, not their separate effects. In the quote from President Clinton, the crucial factor lurking in the background is the performance of the economy. Since the economy experienced vigorous growth during all of Clinton's presidency, separating the effects of welfare reform and economic prosperity on job growth, unemployment, home ownership, and the federal budget surplus is difficult. Aggregate figures cannot disentangle the various effects.

Multivariate Statistical Techniques and Natural Experiments

> In this paper, we exploit a "natural experiment" associated with human reproduction to identify the effect of teen childbearing on subsequent educational attainment, family structure, labor market outcomes and financial self-sufficiency. In particular, we exploit the fact that a substantial fraction of women who become pregnant experience a miscarriage . . . women, who had a miscarriage as a teen, would constitute an ideal control group with which to contrast teenage mothers . . . Our major finding is that many of the negative consequences of not delaying childbearing until adulthood are much smaller than has been estimated in previous studies . . . While teen mothers are very likely to live in poverty and experience other forms of adversity, our results imply that little of this would be changed just by getting teen mothers to delay their childbearing into adulthood.
>
> V. Joseph Hotz, Seth G. Sanders, and Susan Williams McElroy,
> "Teenage Childbearing and Its Life Cycle Consequences: Exploiting
> a Natural Experiment," NBER Working Paper, October 1999.

Further up the hierarchy in figure 2.1, multivariate statistical techniques, such as least squares regression and analysis of variance, are observational techniques that can tease out the separate effects on a variable of interest—say, the effects of child care, age, and education on a woman's decision to work outside the home. These techniques are called *observational* because analysts have no influence on any of the variables involved—they simply take the data as they come from the outside world. (In contrast, as explained below, experimental data are generated when analysts have control over who gets an intervention—such as an experimental job-training program—and who does not.)

My purpose here is to familiarize the reader with the quality of different types of data, not to provide a primer on regression or analysis of variance. But such studies have three notable limitations. First, since individuals are not assigned to the programs randomly, the studies may suffer from "selection bias." Since people voluntarily choose to enroll in a particular program, it may be that those who enroll differ in some significant way from those who don't. For example, if an analyst needs to evaluate a job-training program for low-income mothers, it may be tempting to do so by comparing the outcomes for those who enroll in the program with the outcomes for those who don't. But those who volunteer for the program may be better educated, have stronger work histories, or be better motivated than those who don't volunteer. So the difference in outcomes may be a result of differences in the program participants themselves, rather than any difference caused by the program. Analysts may try to ameliorate this problem by gathering additional information about each participant, but some factors (such as motivation) may be hard to measure.

A second notable problem is that these studies' ability to sort out the separate effects of variable A and variable B on variable C depends upon applying multivariate statistical techniques properly. A whole host of problems can bias the results, from improper sampling and computing procedures to excluding relevant confounding factors. These methodological problems fill academic journals and books, but for our purpose the message is simple—don't put too much faith in any one particular study, because it might contain a mistake. We can only begin to rely on a result when it has been replicated, with other samples, in other contexts, and with other procedures, so that the mistakes that afflict any one study are unlikely to be replicated in the other studies.

A third, related danger with these studies is that they are all based on samples, raising the possibility of sampling error (that is, the particular sample chosen just isn't representative of the population as a whole). In this sense, statistical "proof" is fundamentally different from a proof in mathematics or physics: in those disciplines, the proof answers the question unequivocally, for all time. By contrast, a statistically significant result in one study still leaves open a small possibility that the conclusions are due to oddities in the sample. Again, the answer is to replicate the study, over and over, until we are sure of the results.

A related technique for sorting out the influence of public policy on social problems is the so-called natural experiment. This is not really an experiment in the classical sense of the term—the analyst has no control over who gets a particular program, benefit, or service. Instead, a natural experiment is simply a fortuitous circumstance in which two similar groups exist, differing only by the variable of interest to the researcher.

For example, in the quote above, researchers wished to assess the effect of teenage childbearing on later economic success. But teenage mothers might be different in other ways from teenage girls who don't become pregnant—they might come from families with lower income, lower educational attainment, and less stable marriages. So a straight comparison between women who have children in their teens and women who have children later might not filter out these confounding factors. However, the researchers quoted above managed to obtain work and income data for women who became pregnant but miscarried during their teen years. This group became an excellent "control group" against which to compare teenage mothers, thus isolating the separate effect of teenage childbearing on poverty.

Some uncertainties remain, however, even with natural experiments. First, the problem of sampling error remains, since typically the analyst will study only a small portion of a particular population. Second, since the "experiment" was not designed to assist the researcher, it may not be as "clean" as the analyst might hope. In the example above, what if teenagers who miscarry differ in some consistent way from teenagers who carry babies to term? If miscarriage is affected by drug or alcohol use or by a lack of health insurance, the two groups might not be as similar as the analyst wishes. Once again, the problem of confounding factors weakens our confidence in the results, so that replicating the study in a variety of contexts is necessary.

Experimental Studies (Small and Large)

Conceived and funded by Human Resources Development Canada (HRDC) and managed by the Social Research and Demonstration Corporation (SRDC), SSP offers a temporary earnings supplement to selected single-parent families receiving Income Assistance (welfare) in British Columbia and New Brunswick. To collect the supplement (a monthly cash payment based on actual earnings), a single parent must work full-time and leave Income Assistance. . . . Each of those who [participated] was assigned at random to one of two groups: Members of the program group were given the opportunity to participate in the earnings supplement program; members of the control group were not. Because the two groups are similar in all respects except whether they were allowed to participate in the program, the "impact" or effect of SSP can be measured by the difference between the program and control groups' subsequent experiences. . . . During the first year and a half after program group members were first offered the supplement, SSP successfully increased work, reduced poverty, and reduced welfare dependence.

Winston Lin, Phillip K. Robins, David Card, Kristen Harknett,
and Susanna Lui-Gurr, *When Financial Incentives Encourage Work:*
Complete 18-Month Findings from the Self-Sufficiency Project,
Social Research and Demonstration Corporation, 1998.

As in medicine, the most powerful statistical technique policy researchers can muster is an experimental study. The procedure is conceptually simple. Take all the people you want to study, draw out half the names at random, call that group the "treatment" group, and give them the policy intervention you're interested in. (For example, the analyst might provide them with day care, or better schooling, or higher welfare benefits, or more job training.) Then call the remaining names the "control" group and do nothing but observe them. Over time, by marking the differences between the two groups in performance outcomes (for example, wage income or work days or pregnancy rates), the analyst can determine if the policy intervention works.

This technique is so powerful because it tends to even out the effects of the confounding factors. Is age a factor in wage income? No problem—random selection makes it extremely unlikely that all the older welfare recipients will go into one group, and all the younger welfare recipients will go into the other group. Instead, the age distribution of the two groups will tend to be similar. A similar logic applies to income, race, education, and family structure—all will tend to be similar in the two groups, so the effect of these confounding factors is neutralized. The analyst doesn't even have do know what all the confounding factors are—the process of random selection handles them all.

But even if the procedure is conceptually simple, it is politically and ethically complex. How can we offer higher welfare benefits, or better child care, or superior primary education, to one group and withhold it from another? Despite these problems, the United States has pursued a surprising number of policy experiments. In the 1970s and 1980s, the RAND Corporation conducted a fascinating experiment to learn families' responses to different kinds of health insurance. From 1968 to 1979 the federal government funded a welfare experiment called the negative income tax to find the effects of welfare on work behavior and total income. The experiment was conducted in places as diverse as Denver, Seattle, urban areas of New Jersey and Pennsylvania, rural areas in Iowa and North Carolina, and Gary, Indiana. From 1962 to 1967, the Perry Preschool Program conducted a randomized experiment to determine the effects of high-quality preschool on low-income children. Incredibly, the children in that program, both control and treatment groups, have now been followed through age 40 to determine its long-term effects on welfare use, educational achievement, career success, and criminal activity. A group of prominent academics has identified 27 important experimental studies in areas such as early childhood, primary and secondary education, youth development, crime and violence prevention, substance abuse, mental health, and employment and welfare.[2]

Even the most powerful experimental technique cannot escape the problem of sampling error if the sample size is small. Although treatment and control groups are randomly chosen, there is always the chance that the sample is not representative of the population as a whole. On the other hand, if the sample size is large, we have the best of both worlds: the large sample minimizes sampling error and the experimental technique minimizes confounding factors. Although large-scale experimental studies are unusual, they represent the best possible method for evaluating a policy's effectiveness.

Meta-Analyses and Literature Reviews

> The issue with which research thus far has been most concerned is whether the welfare system encourages female headship. Because benefits are paid primarily to female heads of family with children but with no spouse present . . . the program provides an obvious incentive to delay marriage, increase rates of marital dissolution, delay remarriage, and have children outside of a marital union, all of which will lower the percentage of the population that is married. Virtually any model of marital status and childbearing behavior will have these implications . . . The failure to find strong benefit effects is the most notable characteristic of [the empirical] literature . . . Thus the welfare system does not appear to be capable of explaining most of the long-term trend or any of the recent trend of increasing numbers of female-headed families in the United States.
>
> Robert Moffitt, "Incentive Effects of the U.S. Welfare System: A Review,"
> *Journal of Economic Literature*, March 1992.

Given the difficulties surrounding a single study, the best information we can obtain about a policy often comes from a literature review or meta-analysis. These pieces survey the results from multiple studies, looking for patterns in the results. This eliminates problems with sampling error and also minimizes statistical problems with any one study. But complications and difficulties accompany these procedures. For example, studies with severe methodological problems should be discarded for a literature review, but analysts must not arbitrarily omit studies to suit their own pet theories. Despite these problems, a well-executed summary of the available literature remains an invaluable tool for testing the effectiveness of policy actions. In the quote above, for example, Robert Moffitt explains that although there are theoretical reasons to suspect welfare as a cause of the increase in female-headed households, a review of two dozen empirical studies shows that welfare plays no major role.

Conclusion: Using the Empirical Hierarchy

This chapter is not meant to argue for one methodology to the exclusion of all others. Large-scale experimental tests, for example, are economically, politically, and ethically possible in some contexts but not in others. Also, I do not wish to argue that we should be satisfied with the information or analysis available at a particular time. Constructive policy analysis is an ongoing process of continual improvement in both data and methods of analysis. Rather, my argument is simply that, at any point in time, policy should be based on the best available evidence— that is, information from the highest-possible levels of the hierarchy.

In the chapters that follow, this simple empirical hierarchy will be used to explore two questions:

1. What kind of statistical evidence is being used in policy debates? Is high-quality evidence being used on each side of the ideological divide?
2. After stripping away ideological and theoretical considerations, what does the highest-quality evidence show about policy choices in each area? What can be changed by government policy and what cannot be changed? What are the real choices facing us?

I think you will find the answers surprising. In many cases, the emperor simply isn't wearing any clothes; the hypothesized effects of government policy aren't there. As a result, there is an enormous gap between the policy debates we currently have and the ones we ought to have—the debates we would have if we paid close attention to the quality of our evidence.

3

It's Not the Economy, Stupid!

Why You Shouldn't Vote Your Wallet

Next Tuesday is Election Day. Next Tuesday all of you will go to the polls, you'll stand there in the polling place and make a decision. I think when you make that decision it might be well if you would ask yourself: Are you better off than you were four years ago? Is it easier for you to go and buy things in the stores than it was four years ago? Is there more or less unemployment in the country than there was four years ago?
> Ronald Reagan, closing remarks in the October 28, 1980, presidential debate with Jimmy Carter.

The economy, stupid.
> Sign on the wall of the Clinton campaign "war room" in Little Rock, Arkansas, 1992, attributed to political strategist James Carville.

In February 2004, two widows sat in the Blue Wolf Tavern in Struthers, Ohio, munching cheeseburgers and fries. The talk turned to the coming Super Tuesday primary election, in which John Kerry hoped to sew up the Democratic nomination for president. It wasn't hard to figure out what was on their minds. One of the women, Carol Knafels, said that "Bush has to go! Look at the economy! He promised all these jobs. There aren't any jobs. They went to Mexico, Tunisia, Asia. I've never seen such a mess."

The closed factories in Ohio had more than regional significance. John Kerry won the nomination of his party, but Ohio turned out to be the key to George Bush's reelection. On election night, Kerry conceded defeat after it became clear that Ohio was lost to Bush. And in this crucial state, early polls showed that the economy was the number one issue on voters' minds.[1]

But not everyone in Ohio blamed Bush for the economic conditions in the state. The day after the election, a reporter from the *Washington Post* sat down with a family in northern Ohio to gauge their reaction to the

Bush victory. Cary and Tara Leslie were conservative evangelicals, raising three small children. Cary worked at a car rental business at the local airport, and business had fallen off considerably since the September 11, 2001, terrorist attacks. Mr. Leslie was forced to take a second job delivering pizzas on Friday and Saturday nights, and still watched his income decline by more than one-third. Ms. Cary put their situation this way: "It's been rough. Very rough. I mean scraping by." And yet, Cary insisted that "I don't blame President Bush for anything that's happened with my income. There are jobs out there." Overlooking the Bush record on the economy, the Leslies focused on his religious outlook and moral attitudes.[2]

So who's right here—the widows or the Leslies? The widows would cast the net of presidential responsibility widely, while the Leslies seem to go out of their way to avoid blaming the president for their situation. Traditionally, the American electorate has taken a position similar to the two widows. When Americans cast their votes for president, few things matter more than the state of the economy. Beginning with the New Deal legislation of the Roosevelt administration, Americans have come to expect their leaders to take an active role in economic matters, and presidents are held accountable for their success in maintaining high economic growth and low inflation and unemployment.

Quantitative studies of presidential elections show consistently that the state of the economy contributes greatly to a presidential candidate's success. For example, the high interest and inflation rates of the late 1970s likely contributed to Jimmy Carter's defeat by Ronald Reagan in the 1980 election, and the recession of 1991 and 1992 was a central factor in Bill Clinton's defeat of George H. W. Bush in 1992.

But is it reasonable for us to hold our presidents accountable in this way? They must cope with a huge variety of economic "shocks," including Wall Street booms, bubbles, and busts; oil-price spikes; wars; international currency fluctuations; immigration flows; and banking scandals and panics. What can a voter reasonably expect his or her president to do about short-term economic conditions? Using the highest-quality evidence available, this chapter surveys the existing studies on the macroeconomic tools available to the president and calls for rethinking our expectations about the president and the economy. Despite the popularity of the widows' position, it turns out that the Leslies are closer to the mark: the president can do little about short-term swings in the economy, and we have little reason to blame him or her for temporary slowdowns. Focusing on "the economy, stupid" might have gotten Bill Clinton elected, but it isn't smart voting.

What Does the President Really Control?

To understand the practical limitations faced by the president, we must divide economic policy into two parts: *fiscal policy,* which consists of decisions about taxes and spending, and *monetary policy,* which affects the money supply and the banking system. When they focus on short-term economic effects, economists are generally more sanguine about monetary policy than they are about fiscal policy. Although some economists are doubters, most see monetary policy as a critical tool in stabilizing the economy. Contrary to the main theme of this book, this is one area where government policy does seem to affect behavior.

But don't let that influence your presidential vote. In the United States, the money supply is controlled by the Federal Reserve System, a quasi-public agency with a strong tradition of independence from both the president and Congress. True, the president does appoint members of the Board of Governors of the Federal Reserve, but the appointments are for 14-year terms. What's more, the terms are staggered; in a four-year term, a president is likely able to appoint only two members of the seven-seat board. Moreover, board members cannot be reappointed, so the president cannot use reappointment to sway their votes.

The chairman of the Board of Governors is appointed from among the board members for a four-year term. Conceivably, then, the president could put his stamp on monetary policy through his choice of chairman. Again, however, the reality diverges from the theory. Because the chairman is the spokesperson for the Federal Reserve System, and the stock and bond markets are extremely sensitive to its movements, there is always great pressure to reappoint the sitting chairman to another term to avoid disruption in the markets. So, chairmen tend to serve long terms—an average of 9.75 years since World War II.[3] In practice, then, the average president will be unable to do more than reappoint the current chairman.

Macroeconomics under the First View: The Activism of John Maynard Keynes

If the president can't control monetary policy, what about fiscal policy? Here the theory on what to do is quite clear: every college student in a first-year macroeconomics course can recite the basic tenets of Keynesianism.

While classical economists had emphasized the self-regulating tendencies of unfettered markets, Keynes taught that wage and price rigidities could leave modern economies with lengthy periods of high unemployment. The solution, as Keynes saw it, was for governments to "lean against the wind" and provide extra demand for goods and services in sluggish economic times. The extra demand could be provided by tax cuts, which would presumably raise domestic spending, or by additional government spending on goods and services. In either case, contrary to earlier economic thinking, the government would intentionally run a deficit during a recession or depression. During times of excess demand and inflation, the government would reverse the process, running a surplus by raising taxes or reducing government spending, to put the brakes on the economy.

Keynesianism is a classic example of our first view of economic policy. Faced with an external social failure (wage and price rigidities, leading to sustained underemployment), the government steps in and "solves" the social problem by using its financial powers. The faith of early Keynesians was striking—they truly believed that the business cycle could be eliminated:

> What is needed more than anything else is a mechanism which will enable us to regulate our economy so as to maintain a reasonable degree of economic activity: on the one hand to prevent any considerable unemployment of resources and on the other hand to prevent the stresses of the overemployment of resources and the disorganization that we know as inflation. We need a regulator of employment— a mechanism for the maintenance of prosperity.
>
> The instrument that can do this is as readily available as the steering wheel for automobiles . . . A satisfactory level (or range) or employment must be chosen, and the total rate of spending must be raised when employment is too low and curtailed when employment rises too high. (Lerner 1951, 6)

Debating Automatic Stabilizers

Scholars typically separate their analysis of government spending and tax decisions into two parts. Some changes in the budget happen without explicit direction from the president and Congress; these changes are called *automatic stabilizers*. For example, as the economy slides into a recession, spending on entitlement programs like food stamps and Medicare increases because the number of people meeting the programs' income requirements inevitably grows.

Economists are still divided on the effectiveness of automatic stabilizers. The conventional wisdom is that the growth of the federal budget after World War II has dramatically increased the number and size of automatic stabilizers, helping reduce fluctuations in output, unemployment, and prices. Figure 3.1 illustrates the difference in the cyclical swings in the economy before and after the war.

According to DeLong and Summers (1986), output was three times as volatile before the war as after it. However, in addition to the federal government's growth, the American economy has experienced several other structural shifts since World War II, including a decline in manufacturing, an increase in international trade, and a dramatic increase in the number of women in the workforce. Who knows which of these factors caused the "smoothing" of the business cycle?

Whether or not automatic stabilizers work, a rational voter ought not to consider them in choosing a president. By definition, automatic stabilizers represent things politicians *don't* change to help the economy. Regardless of who is the president, food stamp spending will increase in the next recession and income tax revenues will fall.

Figure 3.1. Annual Percentage Change in Real U.S. Gross Domestic Product, 1901–2007

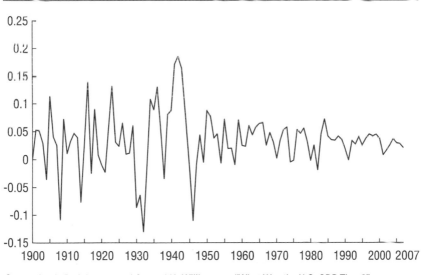

Source: Louis D. Johnston and Samuel H. Williamson, "What Was the U.S. GDP Then?" MeasuringWorth, 2008, http://www.measuringworth.org.

Discretionary Policy: Timing Is Everything

If we are trying to assess whether voters should "vote with their pocket-books," a better way would be to ignore the *automatic* changes in the federal budget and look directly at *discretionary* changes since the Keynesian revolution—the tax and spending changes made explicitly by Congress and the president in response to current economic conditions. But the problem here is that the machinery of the federal government is too ponderous to provide the right economic stimulus at the right moment. The average postwar recession is just 10 months long, making it difficult to time stimulus measures effectively (National Bureau of Economic Research 2008). Congress and the president are like punch-drunk boxers, continually aiming their jabs at the last place they saw their opponent, too slow to realize that the other fighter has already danced away to a new location.

Consider all the steps necessary when the economy slumps into a recession. First, since economic statistics are not gathered instantaneously, but rather take weeks or months to compile, the recession would not be immediately apparent; economists call this the *recognition lag*. In the United States, the acknowledged authority on dating recessions is the Business Cycle Dating Committee of the National Bureau of Economic Research, a group of prominent academic macroeconomists. Over the last five recessions, from 1980 to 2008, the typical delay between the start of a recession and its recognition by the committee was nine months (NBER 2008).

Once the economic threat is identified, Congress and the president must debate the matter and decide on the precise nature of their response. For example, Paul Portney (1976, 245) studied three major tax bills in the 1960s and found that the average congressional delay in passing each bill was 16 months. The combined delay between the beginning of the recession and the passage of remedial legislation (which includes the recognition lag) is called the *inside lag*.

Once legislation is actually passed, it must go through the *outside lag* before the fiscal stimulus takes effect. For example, suppose that Congress and the president decide that a tax cut is in order. When will the bill begin to have an effect on family budgets? If the tax cut is not retroactive, the IRS will need to design and distribute new tax forms and withholding tables, and families will not see the tax cut's benefits until they pay their taxes the following year. Even if the tax cut is retroactive, calculating, printing, and distributing tax rebate checks to all taxpayers takes months. For example, consider the 2001 tax cuts implemented under President George W. Bush.

The president proposed the tax cut during the election campaign of summer and fall 2000, campaigned for it in the fall of 2000, drafted legislation upon taking office in January 2001, managed to get the cuts passed by May 2001, got the first checks into the hands of some taxpayers by late July 2001, and finished sending checks by the end of September 2001.[4]

Thus, while the average postwar recession is just 10 months long, more than 10 months are necessary to implement a stimulative fiscal package. Discretionary fiscal policy is a bit like landing at 1,000-foot plane on an 800-foot aircraft carrier; no matter what you do, you're likely to miss the mark. DeLong puts it this way: "The U.S. government lacks the knowledge to design and the institutional capacity to execute a countercyclical discretionary fiscal policy in response to any macroeconomic cycle of shorter duration than the Great Depression itself" (1996, 47).

The Record on Discretionary Policy

Given the intense political focus on short-run economic conditions, it is surprising that the near-universal consensus reached by empirical studies of discretionary fiscal policy is that the policies haven't worked. For example, Jody Lipford examined the historical record from 1978 to 1998 and concluded that nondefense discretionary spending was "procyclical" in 11 of those 20 years. This means that, rather than leaning against the wind, Congress and the president actually leaned *with* the wind, raising taxes and cutting expenditures during recessions and cutting taxes and increasing expenditures during expansions. On balance, this made the economy more, rather than less, unstable. According to Lipford, "For a spending category arguably most subject to manipulation in the pursuit of macroeconomic policy goals [nondefense discretionary spending], 'getting it right' less than half the time suggests an unwillingness or inability of the Congress, the president, or both to use discretionary spending for stabilization purposes" (1999, 50).

Other scholars have come to similarly pessimistic views about the effectiveness of discretionary fiscal policy. As mentioned in chapter 1, William Keech reviewed postwar economic stimulus packages in 1995 and concluded that *all* of them took effect too late to help aid economic recovery. Drawing on comprehensive studies by Robert Gordon, Lawrence Summers, and himself, Bradford DeLong concluded that "in the post–World War II era, at least, discretionary fiscal policy has given little aid to stabilization, and the degree of countercyclical movement in the federal budget balance has been very close to that which would have been generated by the automatic stabilizers alone" (1996, 47).

The 2008 Recession and the New Deal

The extraordinarily deep and long-lasting recession that began in December 2007 posed unique and urgent questions for policymakers. As of March 2009, the recession had already lasted 16 months, matching the longest of the previous postwar recessions. The length of the recession mitigated the policy lags above; there was much more time to enact stimulative policies before the recession ended. And the depth of the recession, with unemployment reaching its highest rates in nearly three decades, raised the pressure for policymakers to do something. In such an environment, analysts have increasingly turned their attention from the short postwar recessions, focusing instead on the Great Depression as a precedent for policy. After all, didn't Roosevelt pull us out of the Depression by embracing deficit spending and enacting New Deal public works programs? Isn't this a classic example of the effectiveness of Keynesian activism?

Unfortunately, despite what we learned in high school history and college macroeconomics classes, the evidence does not support this simplistic view. In this area, I could not find a literature review or meta-analysis for guidance, but a book by Randall Parker, *The Economics of the Great Depression* (2007), provided the next best alternative. Parker interviewed the 12 most prominent economic historians of the Depression. Among other things, he asked each one of them the following question: "What ended the Great Depression?"[5] Surprisingly, not a single one of the experts attributed the recovery to New Deal programs. Instead, they pointed to the decision to abandon the gold standard, an influx of gold from Europe that expanded the money supply, and the coming of World War II as the sources of recovery. Earlier studies by Brown (1956), Peppers (1973), and Raynold, McMillin, and Beard (1991) also suggest that fiscal policy had little to do with the recovery from the Depression.

However, fiscal policy diehards might contend that we've got our eyes on the wrong example. Perhaps Roosevelt just wasn't consistent enough in his expansionary policies and didn't run large enough deficits to do the job. Under this view, the best exemplar of the possibilities of fiscal stimulus is World War II. Wasn't it the demand for all those planes, ships, tanks, and guns that really ended the Depression?

Unfortunately, this simple argument runs headlong into two severe difficulties. First, we cannot be sure that it was the fiscal stimulus that really righted the economy. Much changed with government spending over the war period: price controls and rationing were instituted, the draft mobilized thousands of young men who might otherwise be unemployed, women entered the workforce in large numbers, and the Federal Reserve expanded the money supply to keep interest rates low and make it easier for the government to borrow money. Since all of these things occurred at virtually the same time as the wartime deficits, it is difficult to show that fiscal policy was the driving force behind wartime expansion. Second, even if fiscal policy is assumed to be effective, the required scale of deficits is daunting. Wartime deficits averaged 18.6 percent of GDP. By comparison, the substantial deficits from 2002 to 2007 consumed an average of just 2.4 percent of GDP (U.S. Office of Management and Budget 2007b). This implies that the deficit would have to be eight times larger than its previous level to be sufficiently stimulative. As discussed in the next chapter, this would require that massive interest costs be paid to foreign investors, causing a drag on growth for many years into the future.

The Empirical Record on Fiscal Policy

A review of the literature on macroeconomics suggests that Keynes may or may not have been right about the theoretical possibilities for government intervention in the economy (see the discussion of Ricardian equivalence below). But a review of the history of Keynesian policy in the United States suggests that Keynesianism is a poor basis for electing presidential candidates. The factors that matter to the economy (monetary policy and automatic stabilizers) are not under short-term control by politicians, while the factors that are under their control (discretionary fiscal policies) have not been proven effective in past downturns and cannot be appropriately timed to jolt the economy when it needs it.

Macroeconomics under the Second View: Keynes and the Loss of Fiscal Discipline

There is, of course, a second-view response to Keynesianism. And consistent with the conservative response in other areas, it suggests that government policy actually makes things worse. Once again, conservatives don't doubt that government policy has powerful effects on the economy; they merely dispute the direction of the effects.

The second view of government fiscal policy was developed by James Buchanan and Richard Wagner and codified in their 1977 book, *Democracy in Deficit: The Political Legacy of Lord Keynes.* Buchanan and Wagner's thesis is that, by providing a legitimate rationale for running deficits, Keynes removed a vital constraint on elected leaders' behavior. Politicians are rewarded for cutting taxes and increasing spending for their constituents and are punished for raising taxes and cutting spending. Since economic conditions are always somewhat uncertain, Buchanan and Wagner argued that politicians would always push for economic stimulus, and Keynesianism would lead to *perpetual* deficits, not just deficits during recessions.

A cursory examination of the data supports Buchanan and Wagner's thesis. The start of the Keynesian age is difficult to pin down precisely, but if we use Buchanan and Wagner's suggestion of the 1964 tax cut, the federal government ran just five surplus budgets until 2004—a batting average of just 12 percent. In the 41 years prior to 1963, excluding World War II, the government ran surpluses in 15 of the remaining 37 years—an average of 41 percent (see figure 3.2).

In other words, while surpluses were almost as likely as deficits before Keynes came along, they have now become rare. Using sophisticated statistical modeling, Kevin Hoover and Steven Sheffrin looked at the relationship between taxes and spending from 1950 to 1989 and concluded that politicians no longer feel the same pressure to raise taxes when they increase government spending:

> There was a change in the causal field or causal relation between taxes and spending which occurred sometime in the late 1960s and early 1970s . . . in the early period, taxes and spending were causally linked . . . in the period following the change in the causal field, taxes and spending were causally independent. (1992, 245)

Deficits, the Crowding-Out Hypothesis, and Inflation

Buchanan and Wagner argue that such continual deficits damage the economy. Since the government must borrow the money to finance these deficits, its actions increase the demand for borrowed money. To get individuals and businesses to lend the additional money, the government must bid up the interest rate for all borrowing. This higher interest rate discourages businesses from borrowing to finance new plant and equipment, and slows economic growth. In this way, government borrow-

Figure 3.2. Surplus or Deficit as a Percentage of Real U.S. Gross Domestic Product, 1919–2007

Source: Author's calculations, based on U.S. Office of Management and Budget (2008) and Louis D. Johnston and Samuel H. Williamson, "What Was the U.S. GDP Then?" MeasuringWorth, 2008, http://www.measuringworth.org.

ing to finance a deficit might "crowd out" private investment, stealing precious funds from their most productive uses.

Buchanan, Wagner, and Barro: Facing Up to the Empirical Uncertainties

As intuitively plausible as the Buchanan and Wagner hypotheses may sound, the truth is that economists have been unable to confirm it empirically. In fact, the data are so ambiguous that a prominent group of economists has argued for a completely different theory, one that seems much less intuitive to ordinary consumers.

Under Ricardian equivalence theory, an idea championed by Robert Barro (1974), government deficits do not raise interest rates because consumers know that the money has to be paid back some day. After all, every dollar the government borrows today must be paid back later, and the government will have to raise taxes or cut expenditures to do it. Wise consumers will anticipate this later event and will adjust their savings plans accordingly. Assuming that consumers have a long-term plan to allocate spending over their lives, they will recognize that government debt will impoverish them in middle or old age, either though higher taxes or reduced government services. Seeing this, rational consumers will therefore increase savings at the time of the initial government deficit by exactly enough to offset the future liabilities. And if everyone in the economy behaves this way, government deficits will not raise interest rates, because the savings supplied by citizens will rise by exactly the same amount as the demand for those savings from government.[6]

So who's right—Buchanan and Wagner, or Barro? Numerous authors have performed statistical tests and have failed to find evidence of the crowding-out effect (Darrat 1990; Evans 1985, 1986, 1987, and 1988; Hoelscher 1983; Motely 1983; and Plosser 1982 and 1987). But the most authoritative source I could find was a review paper by Douglas Elmendorf and Gregory Mankiw in 1998. Mankiw, of Harvard University and the prestigious National Bureau of Economic Research, is one of the nation's most respected macroeconomists and has previously served as the chairman of the president's Council of Economic Advisers. Elmendorf and Mankiw's review was published in the *Handbook of Macroeconomics*, a highly regarded compilation of essays intended to summarize the state of knowledge in the field. At the end of their survey of the empirical literature, Elmendorf and Mankiw conclude that

> this literature, like the literature regarding fiscal policy and consumption, is ultimately not very informative. Examined carefully, the results are simply too difficult to swallow . . . In the end, the empirical literature examining the effects of fiscal policy on consumption, interest rates, and international variables fails to offer clear evidence for or against the Ricardian hypothesis. (1998, 66–68)

A more recent review of the literature by Roberto Ricciuti comes to the same conclusion: "the empirical evidence is inconclusive" (2003, 55). My purpose here is not to debate the theoretical details of crowding out and Ricardian equivalence, but to point out that, even on such a fundamental, basic issue as the effect of deficits on interest rates and prices, economists are unable to determine empirically who is right. Modern macroeconomics, it seems, is theoretically strong but empirically weak. Like a blind and deaf Einstein, economists are able to construct complex, sophisticated, and subtle models of our economy, but are unable to tell which one best represents the real world. We simply don't know whether the deficits created by the Keynesian revolution create higher interest rates.

Conclusion: Rational and Irrational Expectations

The arguments and evidence presented above do not show that the president has no role in economic affairs. As discussed above, most economists believe that the actions of the Federal Reserve have a powerful effect on economic conditions, so the president's choices for the Federal Reserve Board can make a real difference.

But notice that these are typically long-term effects that take place after the president's term expires. By contrast, there is little evidence to show that the president can manage the course of short-term economic events in the way voters seem to expect. Voters unfairly blame the president for economic shocks, such as oil price hikes and fluctuations in international exchange rates, over which he has little control. And the evidence suggests that, at least under current budgeting arrangements, the mechanisms for providing the countercyclical fiscal policy envisioned by Keynes are too ineffective and too slow to stabilize the economy. Although automatic stabilizers may have helped dampen the swings of the postwar economy, the president is not the master of economic events envisioned by proponents of the first view of government policy.

On the other hand, there is also little evidence to suggest that government policy itself is the source of economic difficulties. Yes, the Keynesian revolution may have led to larger and more common federal budget deficits. But contrary to the second view of government policy, we do not have the evidence to show that these higher deficits have led to higher interest rates.

That leaves us with the third view of government policy: that government is neither the cause nor the cure of our economic problems, but rather, like the rest of us, must somehow cope with the ups and downs of the business cycle. At least over the short term, the challenge is not how to control our economic fates, but rather how to best allocate the scarce resources currently available to us. In terms of the five-part catalog of government functions in chapter 1, we ought to be paying much more attention to the redistributional, investment, and service aspects of taxing and spending decisions and much less to changing consumers' and businesses' economic choices. The answer to the voters' dilemma is not to vote with our pocketbooks, because our pocketbooks are not likely to be much affected by the election. The answer is to vote with our hearts or (as economists more coldly put it) with our preference functions. Voting is a way of aggregating preferences, of discovering the choices individuals make under the constraints posed by current circumstances. Which candidate best matches our spending preferences in crucial areas like education, national defense, welfare, and foreign aid? Which candidate's programmatic innovations are most appealing in these areas? In other words, which candidate's priorities for using our limited funds most closely match our own? Voting on this basis allows us to choose from real, rather than imagined, options.

4

Growth Illusions

Can We Spend or Tax Cut
Our Way to Prosperity?

The most influential economic seminar in recent history didn't take place in a university lecture hall or a congressional hearing room. The speaker didn't use a chalk board, a computer, a projector, or a screen. And the seminar's message didn't depend upon historical data, complex mathematical models, or important journal articles. Instead, the most influential economic seminar in recent memory took place in a bar and used nothing but a cocktail napkin.

Here's how Jude Wanniski, one of the participants in the seminar, told the story.[1] Early in the Ford administration, the Republican president had called for an income tax surcharge to fight inflation and reduce the budget deficit. The Republicans fared badly in the midterm elections, losing 48 seats in the House and 4 in the Senate, although it was unclear whether the proposed tax increase or the Watergate scandal caused the disaster. Wanniski, an editorial writer for the *Wall Street Journal* and an admirer of conservative economists Robert Mundell and Arthur Laffer, saw this defeat as an opportunity to introduce the administration to some new economic ideas. He met with Donald Rumsfeld (yes, that Donald Rumsfeld), who was serving as White House chief of staff. Rumsfeld had worked with Laffer in the Nixon administration and admired him. The chief of staff agreed to a meeting with Laffer, Wanniski, and Rumsfeld's top assistants, to allow Laffer to present his ideas.

On the day of the meeting, Rumsfeld had to meet with the president, so Wanniski and Laffer met with Rumsfeld's assistant, Dick Cheney (yes, that Dick Cheney). The seminar took place on December 4, 1974, in the Two Continents Cocktail Lounge of the Washington Hotel, down the street from the White House. During the meeting, Laffer grabbed a cocktail napkin and drew a simple parabolic curve (figure 4.1). Laffer reasoned that every tax increase has both an "arithmetic" and an "economic" effect. The arithmetic effect is the straightforward increase that occurs when higher tax rates are imposed on the same number of economic transactions, and it always has a positive impact on tax revenues. However, the economic effect represents the depressing influence of the tax increase on economic activity, since transactions are now less beneficial for the buyer or the seller or both. The economic effect always has a negative impact on tax revenue. At low rates of taxation, Laffer theorized that the economic effect of taxes was

Figure 4.1. The Laffer Curve

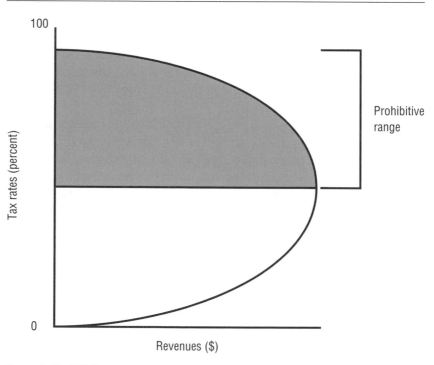

Source: Laffer (2004).

reasonably small, and so the arithmetic effect would dominate the economic effect and a tax increase would raise tax revenues. However, at high rates of taxation, the motivation for transactions would be severely impaired, the economic effect would dominate the arithmetic effect, and a tax increase would actually reduce tax revenue (Laffer 2004).

Using historical examples, Laffer insisted that the United States was on the top half of the curve, so that a cut in tax rates would increase tax revenues. Conservatives loved the idea because it reunited two factions within the conservative movement: fiscal conservatives, who felt that the government ought to run a balanced budget, and libertarians, who felt that the government ought to take as small a share of private wealth as possible. Under this new doctrine of "supply-side" economics, the tension between these factions was eliminated and both sides could push for the same goal: lowering tax rates.

This simple idea, drawn on a napkin in a Washington cocktail lounge, has had a profound impact on policy. In 1981, Ronald Reagan used supply-side economics as the basis for the single largest tax cut in U.S. history (see chapter 5). Supply-side considerations also figured into the Reagan tax cut of 1986, which lowered tax rates for the wealthiest families. In 1996, Robert Dole, the Republican candidate for president, campaigned on a plan for a 15 percent across-the-board reduction in the income tax. His running mate was Jack Kemp, a congressman from New York State who was a prominent advocate of supply-side economics. More recently, the Bush tax cuts of 2001, 2003, and 2005 were all supported by supply-side rhetoric.[2]

Among ardent conservatives, and especially those on Wall Street, supply-side economics remains surprisingly popular. For example, consider the 2006 article "Riding the Right Curve: Laffer Days Are Here Again," by Larry Kudlow, columnist for the conservative weekly *National Review* and host of *Kudlow and Company*, a nightly CNBC broadcast about business and politics.

> It's always amazing to listen to conventional demand-side economic pundits and mainstream reporters who try as hard as they can to minimize the excellent performance of the American economy ever since lower marginal tax-rate incentives were put into place almost two-and-a-half years ago . . . Reagan economic guru Art Laffer taught us thirty years ago that lower tax rates ignite economic growth. Now, the Laffer curve is tracking a business-led expansion that is throwing off record budget revenues while corporate profits are soaring. Profits are the mother's milk of business, the economy, and stocks, and are laying the foundation for even more hefty job gains.[3]

Or consider a speech that same year by Congresswoman Thelma Drake (R-VA) on the floor of the House of Representatives.

In the 25 years before the 2003 tax cuts, economic growth averaged 1.1 percent annually. In the past 3 years, it has averaged 4 percent per year, and the first quarter of this year, we are on track for 5.6 percent for this year. Incredible numbers.

In those 36 months since the tax cuts became law, 5.3 million new jobs have been created. When we talk about Federal tax receipts, they are up 15 percent or $274 billion last year, and when the capital gains tax was reduced from 20 to 15 percent, capital gains tax receipts grew 79 percent from 2000 to 2004.

What has happened with these tax cuts and the reduction to 15 percent is people are making different choices. . . .

Americans are doing that. They are creating new jobs, they are creating new opportunities, and our economy has grown incredibly.

I think that it is important to talk about that tax cuts truly do work. We have often heard it said that if you allow people to keep more of their own money, they will create jobs, they will create investments, they will spend the money. They will use it in our economy, all for the benefit of our Nation. But what we have today is 3 years of solid record to show that that model works.[4]

If Laffer's cocktail lounge seminar continues to be influential, what about its accuracy? After all, popular discussion of taxes and economic growth generally relies on historical examples or macroeconomic aggregates like those used by Congresswoman Drake. And as discussed in chapter 2, such data are low on the hierarchy of statistical evidence, since they fail to account for confounding factors. For example, Congresswoman Drake simply cites aggregate growth rates since the 2003 tax cuts, with some comparison to prior growth rates. But what about other influences on the economy during this time period? What about monetary policy—what was the Fed doing? What was the international economic situation—the exchange rate for the dollar and the trade deficit? Also, shouldn't some adjustment be made for the business cycle? According to the National Bureau of Economic Research (2008), the economy ended its recession in November 2001, so the three years cited by Congresswoman Drake were all in the expansionary part of the business cycle. Is it really fair to compare them to the 25 years prior to 2003, which included both expansions and recessions?

This chapter examines the impact of government policy on long-term economic growth, using higher-order evidence such as literature reviews of multivariate statistical studies. When the inadequacy of raw aggregate statistics is acknowledged and analysis is based on better-quality statistics, the shift in perspective is dramatic. The Laffer curve envisions an easy and painless way to spur the economy—just lower taxes, a move everyone likes. By contrast, the best evidence suggests that the government's influence over economic growth is surprisingly circumscribed, and budget decisions require painful, politically difficult choices between future growth and present economic satisfaction.

The First View: Public Investment in Human and Physical Resources

Liberals do not see high government spending as harmful to the economy; in fact, they point to government expenditures in education, job training, transportation, and research and development as essential to a modern economy. In a House debate on the president's budget on February 16, 2005, Congressman Henry Cuellar (D-TX) gave a typical defense of this position:

> Education has the power to break the cycle of poverty. Education has the power to change lives. As millions of Americans have proven, education has the power to change the future. It has changed mine.
>
> I think the gentleman will agree with me that if we would call, or any Member would call, any economic development foundation in their district and ask them about the importance of a broad-based comprehensive education system, I think they would get the answer, an answer that we all know, that is, there is no greater resource today in our great Nation to attract better jobs with better wages to our communities than a strong education program that we have.[5]

It is certainly possible that individual programs in education, research, and infrastructure development pay long-term dividends in future economic growth. But the evidence suggests that, in the aggregate, we cannot count on public investment to significantly change our economic growth rate, for two reasons: (1) the federal government devotes only a small part of its budget to investment, and (2) the empirical literature on public investment fails to show a clear effect of such investment on economic growth.

The Federal Government and Investment

Every year for more than 50 years, the president's budget has included a breakdown of the investment component of past and future government spending (U.S. Office of Management and Budget 2007a, 55). The figures are surprising, given the public rhetoric devoted to these activities. The Office of Management and Budget, which prepares the president's budget, broadly defines investment. Even so, just 16 percent of the federal government's outlays were devoted to investment in 2006. Furthermore, of that 16 percent, 40 percent consisted of defense investments in ships, tanks, missiles, and other military hardware. Although a fighter jet may well be useful for more than one year, it isn't the kind of investment typically cited by liberal thinkers; among other problems, many weapon systems are produced inefficiently, and changes in operational demands may quickly render some of these weapons unsuitable. That means that the investments usually cited by the left constitute small percentages of the federal budget. Just 3.5 percent of federal outlays are devoted to infrastructure investments like harbors, roads, and bridges, including grants to state and local government. And despite George W. Bush's rhetorical emphasis on education, just 4.4 percent of federal outlays are devoted to education and training, including grants to schools.[6]

The Empirical Literature on Public Investment and Economic Growth

Of course, the theoretical effects of greater spending on education, research and development, and infrastructure are straightforward and easy to grasp. A better-educated worker should be more productive; new, innovative technologies create new products and new markets; and better roads speed the delivery of goods and services. On its face, all of this should raise GDP. However, these models can miss critical elements of public spending in the real world. Since government is not a profit-maximizing institution, it might waste resources on the wrong combination of inputs to produce the desired output. Or public investment might not be well coordinated with private sector activities, so that there is too much of some critical services and not enough of others. Finally, "pork barrel" projects might benefit few citizens.

In 1994, Edward Gramlich published a review of studies on the productivity of infrastructure investments in the *Journal of Economic Literature,* considered the premier journal in economics for such reviews. His article focused on the whether the nation faced an infrastructure shortage such that additional investments would pay high dividends in economic growth.

> As for the alleged infrastructure shortage, the evidence reviewed in the paper is decidedly mixed. The needs assessment approaches and macro time series approaches used to justify big increases in infrastructure spending are flawed in

many ways. One might make some more headway by looking at more disaggregated time series, bond referenda voting, and rates of return, where there is some evidence that some kinds of infrastructure could have been in short supply, but even here the evidence is inconclusive and it is not clear that the overall shortage persists. (1994, 1193–94)

A later article by Etsuro Shioji in the *Journal of Economic Growth* summarizes the literature in a similar way:

> However the empirical evidence on public capital productivity is mixed, to put it mildly. In fact, most of the recent studies on US regional data, especially the ones that employ panel data estimation techniques, do not find public capital to be productive. (2001, 205)

Similar problems plague federal investments in education. The largest federal education programs are Title I grants (which give aid to school districts with disadvantaged children) and student aid for higher education. A 1996 meta-analysis of studies of the effects of Title I on student performance found some modest positive effects but warned that the program was so heterogeneous, with school districts using the money in different ways, that these positive conclusions could not be taken as representative of the entire program (Borman and D'Agostino 1996). A 1997 evaluation of the Title I program for Congress found no indication that the program improved student performance (Puma et al. 1997). A more recent study helped explain these disappointing results. Over time, school districts tend to substitute Title I funds for their local tax revenue, allowing them to reduce tax burdens on property owners. After three years, increases in Title I funds have no discernible effects on school spending (Gordon 2004).

In higher education, Dynarski and Scott-Clayton survey the small literature on the effects of Pell Grants and conclude that "there is little to no persuasive evidence that the Pell Grant program affects college enrollment decisions of young people" (2006, 20).[7] This is probably because the application process for the grant screens out anyone who might be uncertain about attending college. I was unable to find a similar evaluation of the Stafford Student Loan program, but since it uses the same application process as the Pell Grant program, it, too, likely has little effect on college enrollments.

None of this should be interpreted as "investment policy never works." We have not individually investigated the thousands of programs that comprise the U.S. government investment portfolio. Nor have we examined the countless new ideas for innovative programs continually being generated. However, a gulf lies between the confident rhetoric of the left on investment and the reality of marginal effectiveness. While individual programs may work, at present the programs are too small and their effects too limited to alter the aggregate U.S. growth rate.

The Second View: Government as a Drag on Economic Growth

The conservative view of economic growth is simple, straightforward, and easy to grasp. Individuals are motivated by incentives, taxes reduce those incentives, and therefore reducing taxes will increase individual activity and economic growth. By reducing taxes, then, government can unleash the entrepreneurial genie, which can transform our economy. For example, reducing income taxes increases workers' net wages, increasing labor supply, and increases the rate of return on saving, encouraging individuals to save more of their income. With greater labor and capital resources, firms are able to produce more and the economy grows faster.

The problem, of course, is that simple models can omit crucial real-world factors. At least three complicating factors mitigate the simple conservative model: (1) income effects, (2) institutional constraints, and (3) cultural norms.

Income Effects

This one is included in the economics textbooks, but it is often forgotten in the heat of debate. A wage increase or an interest rate increase has two effects. The first, beloved by conservatives, is the substitution effect. As work becomes more lucrative relative to leisure, rational people will substitute more work for some of their leisure. And as financial rates of return increase, those same rational people will substitute future consumption for current consumption, increasing their savings.

However, a second effect, the income effect, actually works in the opposite direction. People with higher wages or higher income from their savings are richer. Richer people, also rationally, can afford to have more leisure and spend more on current consumption. This suggests that higher wages will actually reduce work effort, and higher returns on saving actually reduce saving. Even if the income effect isn't strong enough to overcome the substitution effect, it can substantially reduce the responsiveness of work and saving to changes in taxes.

Institutional Constraints

This one is not included in the textbooks, but ought to be. The textbook model pictures us as casual sellers at a flea market, able to sell exactly as much of our labor and loan exactly as much of our savings as we wish. Each hour of our labor and every dollar of our savings can be separately traded at our whim. But is that really how the world works? Most white-collar workers are paid a salary rather than an hourly wage. Their employers don't keep formal records of their work hours and instead emphasize the workers' performance. Most blue-collar workers are still paid an hourly wage, but they are rarely able to choose exactly how many hours to work. In most occupations, the hours to be worked at the prevailing wage are decided by the employer, not the employee. For example, in fast-food restaurants, retail stores, and manufacturing plants, the firm chooses how many hours to give each employee according to the demand for their products and the costs of labor.

Savings behavior is under similar institutional constraints. Much of our saving is focused on retirement, but that money is often highly regulated by our employers. Our employers decide how much to contribute to our retirement funds—usually a fixed percentage of wage and salary income. Employees can make additional contributions to their funds but these are often limited as well, by our employers or by tax authorities.

Cultural Norms

This one is in the anthropology textbooks but not in the economics or business textbooks. All of our work and savings decisions take place in the context of certain cultural expectations that constrain our choices. Men and women are expected to devote time to marriage, child rearing, and friendship activities—expectations that do not vary much with wages or interest rates. Our consumption habits are conditioned by the behavior of those around us, so that work and saving may be driven by the need to "keep up with the Joneses."

My purpose here is not to develop a full-blown alternative theory of work and savings—that is more than we need here. I mention these three factors simply to make the perhaps surprising empirical results described below more understandable. The empirical evidence is best divided into two parts: (1) studies examining the relationship between growth and the size of the public sector, and (2) studies examining the relationship between growth and taxes.

Growth and the Size of Government

Is there a relationship between the size of a country's public sector and its growth rate? The most extensive study of this type was published by Peter Lindert in 2004, and he found no relationship between social spending and economic growth. Temple summarized the studies in this area in an influential article in the *Journal of Economic Literature* in 1999:

> Among questions that are very important, but likely to remain largely unsettled, that over government size and growth looms large. In political discussion it is common to hear claims that a high ratio of social security transfers to GDP and a high level of government consumption can be damaging to growth prospects. The evidence is not strong. Some researchers find a negative link between government consumption and growth, but overall studies disagree, and it would be wrong to argue that a correlation between small government and fast growth leaps out from the data. (1999, 145)

Growth and Taxes

Garfinkle examined the contention that lower taxes spur growth and found "the empirical evidence supporting this claim to be sparse to nonexistent" (2005, 429). Gale and Orszag similarly reviewed the literature on the Bush tax cuts:

> Empirical studies of the growth effect of actual U.S. tax cuts are relatively rare, in part because the U.S. had only one major tax cut between 1965 and 2000. Feldstein (1986) and Feldstein and Elmendorf (1989) find that the 1981 tax cuts had virtually no net impact on economic growth . . . Cross country studies find very small long-term effects of taxes on growth among developed countries. Mendoza, Milesi-Ferrti and Asea (1997) and Garrison and Lee (1992) find no tax effects on growth in developed countries. Padovano and Galli (2001) find that a 10 percentage point reduction in marginal tax rates raises the growth rate by 0.11 percentage points in OECD countries. Engen and Skinner (1992) find significant effects of taxes on growth in a sample of 107 countries, but the tax effects are tiny and insignificant when estimated on developed countries. (2005, 223)

Among the literature reviews favoring tax cuts, the most cited is the one published by Engen and Skinner in a 1996 issue of the *National Tax Journal.* Even here, however, the effects are small. Engen and Skinner examine a 5 percent across-the-board tax cut in marginal rates, leading to a 2.5 percent cut in average tax rates. In practical terms, this is a large tax cut; the authors describe it as "at the outer fringes of politically feasible reform" (635). However, they found this large tax cut increased long-run growth by only 0.22 percent. Taken together, these three literature reviews (Garfinkle, Gale and Orszag, and Engen and Skinner) suggest that, at least with our current tax structure, the growth effects of tax cuts are small.

As modest as these figures are, even they are overestimates in one sense: tax cuts must be financed somehow. If taxes are financed by cuts in public spending, then the policy change amounts to a reduction in the size of the public sector. As we have seen above, the literature suggests that this does not have much effect on growth. Alternatively, if tax cuts are financed by increased borrowing, we must consider the effect of that borrowing on economic growth. Unfortunately, recent changes in the government bond market have made borrowing to finance tax cuts much less attractive than before.

Americans have been saving less and less of their income over the past 30 years. To make up the difference, the U.S. government has been borrowing more and more of its money from foreign investors. The U.S. Treasury Department reports that in just 10 years, from March 1995 to December 2006, foreign ownership of U.S. government debt more than doubled, increasing from 22 percent of publicly held debt to 54 percent.[8] This is even more dramatic than it might at first appear. Much of the existing debt is old debt, having been held by U.S. institutions and individuals for years. But a tax cut would have to be financed by new debt, which has a different ownership composition than the old debt. In fact, over the 10 years from 1995 to 2006, domestic ownership of U.S. government debt actually decreased, from $2.54 trillion to $1.90 trillion. This means that all of the new debt over these years has been financed outside of the United States.

The practical implications of this change are enormous. Previously, the public debt was a debt we owed ourselves; paying interest and principal payments on the debt meant a transfer from one group of Americans (taxpayers) to another (bondholders). This is like a loan from one member of a family to another; the overall effect on the wealth of the entire family is zero. Now, however, when interest and principal payments on the debt come due, the money leaves our economy. This situation is more like a loan from a credit card company—the debt directly reduces the family's net wealth. This means that any possible growth effects of a tax cut must be weighed against the additional indebtedness incurred in funding the debt: our economy might be bigger, but we own less of it.

Some simple calculations suggest that the debt effects are large enough to wipe out any growth effects from a tax cut. As previously noted, Engen and Skinner estimate that a large tax cut can increase growth by 0.22 percent. They also note that this tax cut would cost the U.S. Treasury about $185 billion dollars (1996, 627). GDP in 1996 was $7.82 trillion (U.S. Bureau of Economic Analysis 2007). If, as suggested above, the debt is entirely financed outside the United States, this means that a growth increase of 0.22 percent of GDP would be purchased with additional debt of 2.4 percent of GDP. Imagine a businessman borrowing money to expand his business but incurring debt payments 10 times the increase in his profits. That is the essentially the situation we face with tax cuts.

Conclusion: Budgeting from the Bottom Up, Not the Top Down

Politicians predict dramatic results from changing government spending and taxes. But the evidence cited above shows that, for far too long, we have been asking the wrong questions about federal government finance. We have been evaluating the federal budget from the top down, asking how it can help us grow faster. The truth is that the budget is the servant of the economy, not its master. Presently, changes in spending or tax revenue have little effect on economic growth.

What we can do, however, is make the most of the resources we have. We need to build the budget from the bottom up, evaluating each program separately, deciding each on its merits. Since government bonds are now owned primarily outside of the United States, we must avoid incurring deficits that increase the debt burden for future generations. Instead, we should consider the tax cost of each program and determine if the benefits exceed the costs. Despite theoretical research and political rhetoric about the macroeconomic effects of the budget, the real choices are surprisingly similar to the microeconomic decisions faced by ordinary families. The current state of the economy dictates our budget, and it is up to us to decide if each item is worth the cost of financing it. The overblown growth rhetoric of the right and the left obscures the actual choices before us. These choices are more straightforward, and more modest, than is commonly acknowledged.

5

A Tale of Two Decisions
Contrasting Standards for Evidence

I n my classes, I spend a lot of time probing the inconsistencies in my students' thinking about public policy. Frequently I find that students, both liberal and conservative, are tripped up in their quest for a consistent public policy worldview by a tendency to view the status quo as "natural" or "inevitable" or "rational." If a policy has been around for a while, the thinking goes, there must be some good reason for it.

In this chapter, I try to show that our current thinking about policy issues is not "natural" or "inevitable" or "rational." I do this by comparing how statistics are used in public policy and in health care. This comparison will, I hope, serve to highlight the rather odd standards we use for evidence in public policy debates.

Decision 1: Reagan's Big Tax Cut

On August 13, 1981, President Ronald Reagan signed the Economic Recovery Tax Act (ERTA)—at that time, the largest tax cut in the history of the United States. The new law

- reduced individual income tax rates by 5 percent in 1981, 10 percent in 1982, and a final 10 percent in 1983;
- reduced the top marginal tax rate from 70 percent to 50 percent;

- indexed the tax brackets for inflation;
- cut the capital gains rate from 28 to 20 percent;
- reduced corporate tax rates; and
- instituted an investment tax credit and accelerated depreciation on buildings, equipment, and vehicles.

The five-year cost of this legislation was estimated at $750 billion (Sloan 1999, 145–46). In addition to its sheer size, the 1981 legislation was important because of its conceptual history: ERTA represented the first victory of supply-side economics.

Remarkably, given the stakes involved, the 1981 tax cut was supported by almost no empirical data. No experimental trials had established the effect of tax cuts on the behavior of American consumers. No multivariate statistical studies supported the claim that lower tax rates would lead to higher tax revenues; in fact, mainstream economists almost uniformly rejected the theory. Henry Aaron, a well-known tax economist at the Brookings Institution, said that "Laffer is the Laetrile of economics," referring to a widely discredited alternative treatment for cancer being used at that time (Sloan 1999, 118). Even conservative economists such as Martin Feldstein, professor of economics at Harvard University and then president of the National Bureau of Economic Research, were skeptical of the Reagan plan. As Feldstein put it, "I think the administration hurt itself by a series of unbelievable statements, starting with those optimistic forecasts about the growth of the economy" (Cannon 1982, 338).

Political observers noted the weak empirical base upon which the 1981 tax cut rested. According to Lou Cannon, who covered the Reagan White House for the *Washington Post,*

> supply-siders believed that these reforms would produce unprecedented economic growth in which . . . increased productivity would generate so much new wealth that government revenues would actually increase. The evidence for this proposition was skimpy, resting chiefly on the disputed outcome of a far more limited tax cut during the Kennedy administration. The supply-siders, however, thought the validity of their economic doctrine self-evident. Many of them expressed their convictions with an evangelical fervor more appropriate for a religious crusade than an economic discussion. (quoted in Sloan 1999, 117)

Even the tax-cut proponents themselves admitted the theoretical, rather than empirical, orientation of their thinking. In a famous interview with William Greider that appeared in the December 1981 issue of the *Atlantic Monthly* and almost cost him his job, David Stockman, the administration's point man on the tax cuts, admitted that "the whole thing is premised on faith, on a belief about how the world works,"[1] that "none of us really understands what's going on with all these numbers,"[2] and that "there was a certain dimension of our theory that was unrealistic."[3]

Another economist asked Murray Weidenbaum, the chairman of the president's Council of Economic Advisers, to provide evidence for the extremely optimistic growth forecasts associated with the administration's tax cut. "What [econometric] model did *this* come out of, Murray?" the skeptic wanted to know. "Weidenbaum glared at his inquisitor a moment and said, 'It came right out of here.' With that he slapped his belly with both hands. 'My visceral computer' " (Sloan 1999, 115).

Of course, it is difficult to show conclusively that Reagan administration officials lacked empirical support for their ideas. Perhaps their sources of information were not revealed to academic specialists or the general public. But the available historical record suggests that, although supply-side economics had a strong theoretical basis, it had a limited empirical foundation. The largest tax cut in the history of the United States, costing three-quarters of a trillion dollars, affecting the fate of the economy and the well-being of millions of Americans, was based on nothing more than a controversial case study centering on one previous tax cut.

Decision 2: Approving the Hepatitis B Vaccine

Three months after President Reagan signed the ERTA, his administration faced a decision on another front. A leading pharmaceutical firm, Merck, Sharp & Dohme, was asking for approval of Heptavax-B, a vaccine for hepatitis B. Hepatitis B is a virus that attacks the liver, and in most cases causes only temporary flu-like symptoms such as fever, nausea, vomiting, fatigue, joint pain, and skin rashes. But in a small percentage of cases, the illness leads to a chronic infection of the liver, cirrhosis, or liver cancer, all of which are severe and life threatening. A hepatitis vaccine might prevent a great deal of misery for those at high risk and might save the lives of many who might otherwise succumb to liver disease. However, the nature of the vaccine made some observers uneasy. Because attempts to grow the hepatitis B virus in the lab had been unsuccessful, the new vaccine was made from the blood of infected individuals. The virus had been deactivated through heat or chemical means, but the idea of keeping healthy people healthy by injecting them with the blood of the sick seemed risky.

Fortunately, FDA Commissioner Arthur Hayes Jr. had very good information on which to base his decision. Like all vaccines and drugs under the FDA's jurisdiction, the new vaccine had undergone testing with both animal and human subjects. Heptavax-B was first tested for safety and efficacy in chimpanzees and then in a group of more than 200 human volunteers from Merck.

But because the chimpanzee or human subjects could have been unusual in some way, the FDA required much more stringent statistical information to prove the vaccine's value: a full-scale double-blind clinical trial in which subjects were randomly assigned to receive either the vaccine or an innocuous placebo shot. Only then could the effects of the vaccine be fully separated from other factors (such as age, previous health history, or health habits) that might affect whether a person contracts hepatitis B. In the late 1970s, epidemiologist Wolf Szmuness, whose wife had nearly died from hepatitis B, conducted exactly such an experiment.

Because hepatitis B can be contracted through sexual contact, and because gay men typically have more sexual partners than heterosexual men or women, gay males represented an ideal test population for the vaccine. Szmuness, the head of epidemiology at the New York Blood Center, sought the cooperation of New York's gay community. Szmuness and his colleagues eventually recruited 1,083 participants. Each had to pass a blood test to ensure that he did not have hepatitis B at the beginning of the experiment. Then the participants were given coded numbers and randomly assigned to receive either three vaccine injections or three placebo shots over six months. Neither the participants, nor the doctors giving the shots, nor even Szmuness himself knew which participants received which injections—only two safety officials on Szmuness's staff did.[4]

The participants were to be followed for two years afterward, taking blood tests for hepatitis B every three months. Through the hard work of Szmuness's staff and the gay community's dedication, about 90 percent of the participants completed the entire series of blood tests. Only when all the blood tests were completed and the health status of each participant was cataloged did the team break the code and compare disease rates for the vaccine and placebo groups. The vaccine turned out to be safe and remarkably effective: 92.3 percent effective for high-risk men.[5]

With such high-quality statistical data (data from the top of the statistical hierarchy in chapter 2) Commissioner Hayes could confidently isolate the separate effect of the vaccine on the health of those who might receive it. The Heptavax-B vaccine was approved by the FDA on November 16, 1981, and Commissioner Hayes recommended that the vaccine be taken by high-risk individuals such as health care workers and persons with numerous sexual partners.[6]

Comparing the Decisions

What is truly remarkable about these two decisions is the asymmetry in the information mustered to support them. On the one hand, the Reagan tax cut was supported by information at the bottom of the statistical hierarchy from chapter 2—a single, disputed case study. On the other hand, the FDA required statistical data of the highest order to approve the Heptavax-B vaccine: controlled, double-blind experimental data from large-scale tests on human beings. Why are our expectations so different in these two cases? To highlight the contrast further, consider what would have happened if the type of data and analysis had been switched. If Merck had submitted the kind of data used by Reagan and Stockman in a vaccine approval request, the application would have been quickly dismissed, and the scientists involved would have suffered serious blows to their professional reputations. No epidemiologist with any standing in the medical community would suggest approving a vaccine based on a trial on a single individual—but that is essentially what the Reagan administration did with the ERTA.

One explanation for the difference between the two decisions might be an inherent difference between the two situations. Isn't it just impossible to put the country through the kind of experimentation used in the hepatitis vaccine? Wouldn't it be incredibly unfair, for example, to randomly divide taxpayers into two camps and give one camp a lower tax rate, just to test their reactions to tax cuts?

While double-blind clinical trials are probably impractical in tax policy, it does not automatically follow that we must resort to the lowest form of statistical evidence. Plenty of high-quality statistical techniques are still available from the top of the statistical hierarchy (figure 2.1). For instance, tax rates have fluctuated during various presidential administrations, depending upon the nation's financial needs and the interest groups holding influence. We can correlate these different historical tax rates with tax revenues and national growth rates over time to observe how tax revenues and growth rates react to changes in tax rates. What's more, statistical techniques such as multiple regression can help isolate the effect of taxes from the countless other variables that might affect national growth rates—exchange rates, national budget surpluses and deficits, changes in demographics, and so on. Admittedly, these techniques are not as powerful in controlling for confounding factors as double-blind experimentation, but they are considerably more powerful than mere case studies.

An additional powerful device for predicting the likely effect of tax cuts is datasets of individual taxpayers. Taxpayers vary in the rates they pay, based on their income, their state and city, their family's size, their investments, and so on. Those individual differences in tax rates can be correlated with their work, spending, and saving habits to demonstrate the effect of tax cuts on their behavior. Of course, individuals vary in their work, spending, and saving patterns for a wide variety of reasons, but once again, statistical techniques are available to separate the effect of taxes on behavior.

The Use of Statistics in Public Policy Decisions

By themselves, these two case studies provide only weak evidence that policy decisions are poorly grounded in empirical realities. It would be ironic to use case studies alone to argue that politicians use weak empirical methods! Case studies make the differences between public policy and medicine tangible and memorable, but they must be backed up by more comprehensive evidence.

How unusual are the contrasting examples I have just described? Is there really a difference in the quality of evidence used in medicine and public policy, or are these just isolated stories? Chapter 2 described a hierarchy of statistical information, with higher-quality information at the top of the pyramid. How far up this hierarchy do typical debates in medicine or politics take us?

Few citizens are capable of reviewing the literature on the negative income tax experiments of the 1960s and 1970s, or the RAND health insurance experiments of the 1980s, or the Head Start experiments of the 1970s, but they trust their elected representatives to evaluate this information. Legislators communicate with each other in committee meetings and on the floors of the legislative houses—discussions captured in publications like the *Congressional Record*. But here the debate is strikingly nonquantitative. Simple case studies, anecdotes, raw figures, and percentages abound. The *Congressional Record* for the 106th Congress (covering the regular sessions in 1999 and 2000) reveals that, out of the thousands and thousands of pages of print in this daily publication, there was not a single mention of the terms "statistically significant" or "t-tests." The terms "standard deviation" and "statistical regression" appeared just four times in the whole of those two years; the term "statistical significance" appeared just three times; and the term "controlled experiment" appeared just twice. Moreover, almost all of these cases involved the testimony of expert witnesses before Congress—not speeches made by members of Congress themselves. Often, much of this testimony is simply placed in the record without being actually read or spoken before a congressional committee, so we can't say for certain that members of Congress ever heard these terms being discussed.

The *Congressional Record* is just one possible source of statistical data for policymakers; certainly, they might obtain such information from other sources. But more systematic information about statistical use in policy analysis is also available. A large literature has emerged to examine the use of policy analysis, including statistical analysis, by political actors. Its consensus is that politicians make surprisingly little use of policy analysis (see, for example, Davidson 1976; Frye 1976; Jones 1976; Mooney 1991; National Research Council 1968; Weiss 1989; and Whiteman 1995). The prevailing view is that, because politicians and policy analysts have different goals and perspectives, they live in two different "cultures" with little effective interaction between the groups (Nelson et al. 1987). As one analyst puts it, we are witnessing a "retreat from analysis in public life," "a triumph of postmodern sensibility in the domain of policy," and "a focus on the telling of anecdotes rather than on policy substance" (Kirp 1992). Thus, unlike in medicine, much of our discourse and decisionmaking in policy appears to be based on evidence from the bottom third of the statistical hierarchy (figure 2.1).

A recent study by three scholars from the University of Maryland helps illustrate this. Beginning in the late 1980s, states were allowed to experiment with alternative welfare systems. Three such experiments were particularly noteworthy: the Greater Avenues for Independence (GAIN) program in California; the Child Assistance Program (CAP) in New York; and Florida's Project Independence. Greenberg, Mandell, and Onstott (2000) interviewed 98 mid- and high-ranking welfare officials from 41 states about their knowledge of these experiments. The authors found that, although state officials knew about the welfare experiments, they had little interest in their actual outcomes—whether or not the programs worked. As Greenberg and his coauthors put it, "in no instance were estimates of the effects of the tested programs, presumably the *raison d'etre* for conducting random assignment experiments, decisive in the decision to adopt or not to adopt a tested policy" (2000, 380). Instead, the welfare officials were primarily interested in the programs' logical consistency (whether they *should* work), in the public's acceptance of or resistance to the programs, and in whether the programs were consistent with federal oversight requirements.

Recently, there has been increased interest in the United Kingdom in promoting what is called *evidence-based policy* (Nutley, Davies, and Smith 2000). The most visible result of this effort is the Campbell Collaboration, which serves as a kind of clearinghouse and coordinating body for high-quality, systematic evaluations of policy interventions. In the United States, a beachhead in the battle for sound policy has been established by the Coalition for Evidence-Based Policy. Founded in 2001, this nonprofit group headed by prominent academics and government consultants has had some success in persuading officials at the Department of Education, the Department of Justice, and the Office of Management and Budget to adopt more rigorous procedures for empirical review of proposed policies. This effort has affected programs as diverse as math and science education, home visits by nurses, and the reintegration of ex-offenders into their communities. However, an independent evaluation of the group's work warns that "it is too soon to know with any certainty whether evidence-based program evaluation will be widely accepted and endure as an integral component of policy and practice in the Executive branch and the Congress" (Martin 2004).

The Use of Statistics in Health Care

It is relatively easy to characterize the evidence health care professionals use to make decisions. Few citizens have the statistical knowledge to evaluate medical experiments, but they trust that their doctors will do it for them. Doctors communicate with one another extensively through medical journals, and in recent years a cottage industry has formed around analyzing the statistical techniques used in medical journals. Typically, the analyst will sample a number of articles in a particular field of medicine and summarize the statistical techniques used. The most influential article in the field appears to be Emerson and Colditz's 1983 analysis of statistical techniques used in the prestigious *New England Journal of Medicine*. Others include the following:

- Weiss and Samet's (1980) assessment of statistical use in 585 articles in six of the best-known general medical journals;
- Reznick, Dawson-Saunders, and Folse's (1987) analysis of the statistical techniques used in 200 articles from four surgical journals;
- Rosenfeld and Rockette's (1991) examination of the use of statistics in a sample of otolaryngology journals;
- Juzych and coauthors' (1992) work on statistical use in three ophthalmology journals; and
- Cardiel and Goldsmith's (1995) review of randomly selected articles from each of eight journals in internal medicine and rheumatology.

The results of these studies are generally consistent. Many of the articles examined—somewhere between 19 and 72 percent—used no statistics or only descriptive statistics such as the mean, median, or standard deviation (see table 5.1). Another large percentage of the articles—somewhere between 28 and 81 percent—used a wide variety of inferential statistical

Table 5.1. Studies of Statistical Use in Medical Journals

Authors	Date	Medical journals examined	Studies found to use inferential statistics (%)
Weiss and Samet	1980	Six general medical journals	45
Emerson and Colditz	1983	*New England Journal of Medicine*	42
Reznick et al.	1987	Four surgical journals	55
Rosenfeld and Rockette	1991	Four journals in otolaryngology	28
Juzych et al.	1992	Three ophthalmic journals	42
Cardiel and Goldsmith	1995	Eight journals in rheumatology and internal medicine	81
Mean			49

Source: Author's calculations.

techniques.[7] To summarize across all medical journals, about half of the articles used inferential statistics. Two of the studies (Juzych et al. 1992 and Rosenfeld and Rockette 1991) looked at statistical use across time, and found that the use of statistics is becoming more common and the statistical techniques are becoming more sophisticated.

These surveys of statistical use in medical journals often include a great deal of hand-wringing over the misuse of statistics in articles and physicians' need for more statistical training (see, in particular, Reznick et al. 1987 and Weiss and Samet 1980). Nevertheless, approximately half of the journal articles in medicine are in the top two-thirds of our technique pyramid (figure 2.1). What's more, the medical community appears to expect that the quality of statistical techniques should and will improve in the future. Rosenfeld and Rockette put the situation this way:

> This study suggests that the prevalence of analytic studies and inferential statistics in otolaryngology journals is increasing . . . A consequence of these trends is that a greater level of statistical expertise will be expected of future writers and readers of the otolaryngology literature. Ideally, this could be achieved through post-graduate courses integrated into national meetings, residency programs, and research fellowships. (1991, 1176)

Suppose you visited a doctor after learning, God forbid, that you had cancer. Suppose further that the doctor, although aware of the *theoretical* possibilities for treatment, was unaware of the *empirical* probabilities for success of those treatments. He might tell you that, theoretically, surgery could cure the cancer, if the cancer hadn't spread, if the surgeons got all of it, and if you didn't die on the operating table. And yes, he might go on, chemotherapy could be helpful, if administered properly, if your type of cancer responded to this treatment, and if the treatment itself didn't kill you. And finally, radiation therapy might help, if the radiation could be directed at the appropriate place, if the tumor were the type to be affected by radiation, and (again) if the radiation itself didn't make you terminally ill.

Imagine your frustration with such a doctor. "What do the experts say to do?" you might ask him. "Well," he might reply, "the experts disagree. It may be some time before they come to agreement on the proper treatment. Until then, it's up to you to decide what to do." In anger or in tears or both, you might well say something like, "But I don't have time for all those experts to agree with each other! I have to make a decision now, based on the evidence we have. What does the best available evidence suggest we should do?"

This example might seem farfetched, but it closely approximates the interplay between economists and policymakers. Economists are steeped in an academic culture that values theoretical sophistication over empirical magnitudes (see chapter 8). Harry Truman complained about economists who constantly said "on the one hand . . . on the other hand." "Give me a one-handed economist!" he cried out in frustration (Boller 1981). This leaves politicians and the public free to make their decisions based on ideology, or intuition, or political expedience.

Returning again to our medical analogy, suppose alternatively that your doctor made his recommendations based on ideology rather than empirical considerations. "I believe in chemotherapy," he might say; "I don't believe in surgery. In fact, I'm active in a national organization—Physicians for Chemo—that advocates the use of chemotherapy for all cancers, and works to restrict the number of surgical beds in major hospitals. Surgery is a form of human mutilation, plain and simple! My father, a physician, was also a good chemo man, and all my physician relatives are chemo men and women. In fact, this whole county is chemo country, and we're working to eliminate all surgeons from the boards of trustees of county hospitals."

Wouldn't the consistency and vehemence of the doctor's beliefs concern you? Why should the solution to all types of cancer be the same? Your worries would be similar if the doctor were a rabid surgery advocate, or a dyed-in-the-wool radiation man. For you, chemotherapy, surgery, and radiation are only means to an end—getting well. You have no allegiance to the method of getting well—only to the method that works best for you. Adopting a particular doctor's ideology means abandoning a possible weapon in your arsenal against cancer—a weapon that may prove most effective in your fight. What you'd need would not be a fixed ideology, but an open mind and reliable information to guide your choice.

Again, this example is purely hypothetical because such a narrow-minded doctor is hard to imagine. But is it easy to imagine analogous circumstances in the public arena. Conservatives argue for restraining government intervention across the spectrum of issues: in welfare, in health care, in taxation, in regulatory policy, and in Social Security. Liberals support an expansion (or at least, maintenance) of the government's role in all of these areas. Why does the doctor's position seem so strange, and the positions of conservatives and liberals seem so natural, when they are so similar? I would argue that one important difference is that in the medical case, at least some of the key decisionmakers (doctors) have statistical training, while in the case of public issues, the most important decisionmakers (politicians and the public) do not.

Even if most doctors do not engage in experimental trials, their statistical training exposes them to a set of practical rules about the quality of the empirical data they encounter. They know, for instance, that a random, double-blind, placebo-controlled study is superior to a single case study. Of course, through overwork, incompetence, or lack of effort, doctors do sometimes take shortcuts and prescribe treatments based on hearsay and intuition. But teaching statistics to doctors makes the standards for evidence clear to all, and those standards guide medicine's long-term development. While a particular doctor may depend upon his limited clinical experience with a few patients, no one argues that this is the appropriate way to guide medical decisions; doctors share a commitment to make decisions according to the best available evidence. By contrast, no similar commitment is shared by politicians and the public. Without training in statistics, all empirical evidence seems equally valid and disagreements among conflicting statistics cannot be resolved. Instead, statistical evidence becomes a decoration, a window dressing, for arguments based on other considerations.

Conclusion: The Importance of the Difference

My point is not to explain the practical reasons why we treat medicine differently from public policy.[8] Rather, I simply want to illustrate the inconsistencies in our thinking between the two fields. Our differential treatment of public policy and health care reveals a gap in our logic. Political scientists are fond of pointing out the advantages gained when elites distort information and the public has limited comprehension of that information. While the political system undoubtedly provides inaccurate and, perhaps, biased data, the question is why citizens, analysts, and journalists don't push for policy information that is as least as good as the medical information they demand. If it makes sense to seek out high-quality statistical information to make informed medical judgments, why does it seem natural to make policy decisions based on anecdotes? If we embrace statistics and controlled experimentation for health choices, why take a casual, intuitive approach to policy choices? Both medicine and policy analysis require complex, multicausal analysis to separate the effect of interventions from other confounding factors.

Both fields raise profound and troubling ethical issues. And both fields demand answers to important challenges that affect real people. If it is important to provide a single mother with the right medical treatment for diabetes, isn't it also crucial to provide her children with a decent education or to provide her with streets where she is protected from physical assault? If both fields are important and complex, why does it make sense to apply different standards of evidence to each one?

As noted at the beginning of this chapter, we tend to believe that the status quo is inevitable and optimal. The health care comparison shows that our current approach to public policy is neither. Decisions based on a higher order of evidence are possible; medical professionals make them every day. Given the wrenching decisions that must be made in the public sector, we cannot afford to use anything less than the best possible evidence.

6

Is Education the Great Equalizer?

Few issues preoccupy American voters and politicians more than education. What sets it apart from other issues is that it cuts across all levels of government. It is continually among the top issues in any presidential or congressional campaign; it is the most expensive, and often most controversial, item in state government budgets; and it typically dominates the politics of small and medium-sized towns. And education is the one government service considered so important that we routinely set up entirely separate units of government (independent school districts) to provide it.

Given all the attention paid to education, then, it is surprising that findings from the empirical literature surrounding education are not commonly known. What follows is a review of that surprising literature, concentrating on the issue of educational equity. Most Americans, I think, would agree with the principle that poor kids ought not to be disadvantaged in life just because of the circumstances of their births. Our tacit assumption is that the current education system "levels the playing field" and provides opportunity for all. However, the empirical literature in this area follows the pattern established in previous chapters of this book: claims about the efficacy of the current system and of reform strategies are routinely inflated. A review of the limitations of current education policy suggests that we ought to be more open to new ideas and more sensitive to the additional inequality brought about by some education reforms. It also suggests that we ought to become more understanding about the need for long-term support for the disadvantaged.

Education as "the Great Equalizer"

The first view of education policy, the liberal view, is that schools can serve as "the great equalizer." Although students may not begin school with the same backgrounds and cultures, a common educational experience will provide all with an opportunity to succeed. If schools are not effective, then additional resources, such as more teachers, higher teacher salaries, more computers, and additional classroom space, will produce better outcomes. Like well-organized factories, schools that provide better inputs will produce better student achievement outputs.

The Coleman Report

James S. Coleman struck the initial blow to the first view in 1966. In the Civil Rights Act of 1964, Congress asked for a study to examine differences in educational opportunity by race, religion, and national origin. The expected result was that such a report would confirm widespread discrepancies in educational resources and would culminate in a request for a large federal program to redress these imbalances. Instead, Coleman's report (U.S. Office of Education 1966) provided surprising answers. After a massive study involving surveys of 600,000 students in 3,000 schools nationwide and controlling for a wide variety of factors affecting student achievement, Coleman concluded that educational resources were not as unequal as previously thought. Much more surprisingly, Coleman found that school-related educational resources—teachers, classroom space, books, and so on—had little influence on student outcomes.

According to Daniel Patrick Moynihan and Frederick Mosteller, who summarized Coleman's work for a Harvard seminar in 1968, the results showed that less than 1 percent of the variation in educational outcomes could be attributed to differences in per pupil expenditure (cited in Kahlenberg 2001, 54). School resources did have a stronger effect on minority children than on white children. However, what really mattered for educational achievement, according to the report, was a student's family background—his or her parents' income, education, and values. The backgrounds of other students in the school also mattered, although they were less important than the student's own background.

Does Money Matter?

Coleman's conclusions have been confirmed by numerous studies since the 1966 report. In fact, by the 1980s, education researchers had begun to wonder whether school resources had any effect at all on student performance. In a series of influential papers in the 1980s and 1990s, economist Eric Hanushek, then of the University of Rochester, argued that, at least under current arrangements, higher teacher salaries, smaller class sizes, higher per-pupil spending, and other additional resources have no effect on student test scores or graduation rates. Hanushek reviewed dozens of statistical studies and concluded that "throwing money at schools" has little effect, because schools have little incentive to operate efficiently (see, for example, Hanushek 1997).

Hanushek's conclusions have been hotly contested by education researchers who believe that his method of aggregating and summarizing previous studies is flawed. These researchers have found significant relationships between student performance and school characteristics such as per-pupil expenditures, teacher education, teacher experience, teacher salary, teacher-pupil ratio, and school size (see, for example, Greenwald, Hedges, and Laine 1996). As a result, the question "does money matter?" has become a central debate in the educational research literature.

Size Does Matter

But notice how far the debate has strayed from the liberal worldview. The current debate is whether school inputs have *any* demonstrable influence at all on student performance, not whether schools provide equal educational opportunity. As educational scholars have developed more and more sensitive means for detecting the influence of school variables, some have found measurable effects. But such findings say nothing about the size of the effects, and researchers have found that school variables have disappointingly small effects on student behavior. In other words, the literature does not contest Coleman's conclusion that community, family, and student background have a much larger effect on students than school variables.

A meta-analysis of the literature by Greenwald and his coauthors (1996) estimates the magnitude of the effects of school changes. Because the original studies used widely different units of measurement (dollars, years of teacher experience, test scores, numbers of students), the estimates are "normalized" by converting all variables to standard deviation units. While this may sound technical, the process is actually quite straightforward. Take, for example, the average teacher salaries for each school district in a state. Those average teacher salaries will vary from one district to another—some suburban districts will pay high salaries, while some urban and rural districts will pay low salaries. The standard deviation is a measure of how widely average teacher salaries vary from one school district to another; a large standard deviation indicates that school districts vary a great deal in teacher salaries from one district to another, while a small standard deviation indicates that teacher salaries are pretty much the same in all districts.

Greenwald and his coauthors report their results in standardized regression coefficients, or the typical change caused by a one standard deviation increase in one variable, when the resulting change in student performance is also measured in standard deviation units. To illustrate using teacher salary, a standardized regression coefficient of two would mean that one standard deviation increase in teacher salaries would typically result in a two standard deviation increase in student performance.

Unfortunately, none of the effects reported by Greenwald and his coauthors are anywhere near as large as in this example. To minimize the effect of unusual studies, the authors report the median standardized regression coefficient from all studies available for each of the school variables. They report that the largest effect is due to teacher experience, where one standard deviation in teacher experience results in a .0984 standard deviation increase in student performance in studies since 1970.[1]

In contrast, the effects of socioeconomic status on achievement are considerable. Because factors like race, income, and family structure are highly correlated, we must consider the combined effect of these factors on student performance. The New Jersey Department of Education has developed an index of socioeconomic status for school districts that takes into account parents' average education level and typical occupation, the average number of persons in a student's family, median income and unemployment in the community, the percentage of residents below the federal poverty level, and whether the community is urban.

Using this index and controlling for school factors such as expenditures and district size, Walberg and Fowler (1987) reported a median standardized coefficient on socioeconomic status of .656. In other words, a one standard deviation change in socioeconomic status was associated with a two-thirds of a standard deviation change in student performance—an effect more than six times as big as the most powerful policy variable, teacher experience.[2] A later study by the same authors, which also controlled for other school characteristics such as teacher-pupil ratio, average teacher salary, and teacher education, reported a standardized coefficient of .522 for socioeconomic status.[3]

The same general conclusion, that socioeconomic factors are more powerful in predicting academic performance than school-related variables, is supported by other studies that don't report standardized regression coefficients. Sutton and Soderstrom (1999) report that demographic factors explain three times as much of the variance in Illinois test scores as school policy variables.[4] Caroline Hoxby uses the same multivariate statistical procedure and finds that family variables explain 11 to 14 times as much as school inputs and neighborhood variables *combined*. Hoxby concludes, "there is substantial evidence that his or her family is the most important determinant of a student's outcomes" (2001, 95).

Government as the Problem, Vouchers as the Solution

The second view of education policy, the conservative view, is that students are being held back by bureaucratic inefficiencies in our school system. The answer, then, is to refocus schools on student performance by eliminating bureaucratic structures and substituting market-like mechanisms that give parents the opportunity to choose the schools right for their children (Chubb and Moe 1990). Instead of funding schools, money would be given directly to parents as a school voucher that would pay tuition at a school of the parents' choice. The school would then redeem the voucher for cash from the government. Under this scheme, all schools would essentially become private schools, but public funding for schools would continue through parental choices. Competition for students would then force underperforming schools to improve.

Although educational vouchers strike many people as unnatural, there are many good examples of similar arrangements in other fields. After World War II, the G.I. Bill gave returning veterans a voucher (although that term was never used) for almost any college or university in the country. The Food Stamp program gives vouchers that can be redeemed at any grocery store. And Medicare gives senior citizens a voucher for health care that can be "redeemed" at participating hospitals and physicians' offices.

John Chubb and Terry Moe helped revive the concept of educational vouchers with their influential 1990 book, *Politics, Markets, and America's Schools*. Their rationale for vouchers fits perfectly into the second view that government itself is the cause of policy problems. According to Chubb and Moe, the effort to keep school districts democratic and publicly responsible has turned schools into political institutions that seek to balance the interests of teachers, unions, and administrators with those of students. This political balancing stifles innovation and improvement, and causes schools to forget their "bottom line"—their students' academic success. The way to break this deadlock, Chubb and Moe reason, is to give all power over resources directly to the ultimate consumers of educational services—the families. Because those families want the best for their children, they will keep the system focused on academic achievement.

The earliest empirical work on the effectiveness of vouchers simply compared the outcomes of public and private schools, and concluded that the latter were generally more effective. But this approach has been widely criticized because it fails to control for differences between public and private school students' family backgrounds. If private school students are richer and have better-educated and more involved parents, they will tend to do better even if the school itself is no more effective than a public school. And even if observable characteristics like race, income, and parents' education are statistically controlled, unobservable characteristics such as parental involvement and expectations still lurk as possible confounding factors, making it difficult to determine whether vouchers actually improve learning.

Another approach used by researchers is to examine the competitiveness of existing school environments. If a metropolitan area has a greater number of school districts per capita, parents have greater choice over where to reside and send their children to school; and if a metropolitan area has a greater number of private schools per capita, parents also have more educational choices. More choice, so the argument goes, should lead to a more competitive environment and better-educated students. So the studies using this approach compare metropolitan areas with greater and lesser degrees of school competition, looking for differences in standardized tests.

The studies using this approach have reached mixed conclusions. In a series of articles, Hoxby (2000) has shown that greater competition is associated with higher academic performance. However, Robert McMillan (2001) has found that additional private schools do not spur public schools to do better, and Christopher Jepsen (2002) has come to the same conclusion. One great difficulty of this approach is that causality may run in the opposite direction than originally anticipated: competition may affect school performance but school performance may also affect competition, because poorly performing schools may encourage the creation of private schools and may cause voters to resist school consolidation. Therefore, a comparison between metropolitan areas examining school competition and student performance may not measure what we want it to measure. There are statistical methods to address this problem, but they are generally regarded as imperfect (Gill et al. 2001, 112).

The Voucher Experiments

Given the problems with more indirect measures, the best available data come from the voucher experiments recently conducted around the country. The best-analyzed private voucher experiments were performed in Charlottesville, Virginia; Dayton, Ohio; New York City; and Washington, D.C. In these programs, a private foundation provided partial scholarships to private schools (including religious schools) for qualifying low-income families. Since the foundations could not provide funding for all the families that applied, a lottery was held for the available scholarships and the families not chosen were utilized as a control group. Both groups completed extensive questionnaires concerning income, race, parents' education, and so forth.

The only *public* voucher programs have been conducted in Milwaukee, Wisconsin; Cleveland, Ohio; and the state of Florida. The Milwaukee and Cleveland programs were similar to the New York City, Dayton, and Washington programs, except that funding was provided by the states. Although the Milwaukee program was initially limited to nonreligious private schools, both programs now include religious schools and the vouchers are awarded by lottery if the demand for scholarships exceeds available funding. However, the Cleveland program did not include provisions to gather data from families not chosen, and in the Milwaukee case the vouchers available exceeded the number of applicants, so finding an appropriate control group was more difficult.

The Florida voucher system is unique and more difficult to analyze. The State of Florida grants vouchers to students whose schools have received an F on the state's evaluation scale for two consecutive years. The students are not required to leave their public schools but are given a limited scholarship to attend the private or religious school of their choice. So far, however, few schools have been given Fs for two years in a row, and few students have chosen to use their vouchers, frustrating analysis. In addition, the program provides no natural control group, making comparisons difficult.

The achievement effects of these voucher programs have been the subject of some controversy, with Paul Peterson and his colleagues arguing that vouchers work (see Greene, Howell, and Peterson 1998 and Greene, Peterson, and Du 1998) and a variety of other researchers (including John Witte 1998 and Kim Metcalf and coauthors 1998) finding no significant difference between voucher students and control groups. Gradually, however, the scholars have come to a consensus: if vouchers work, they appear to work consistently only for low-income African American students. The best available survey of this literature, by researchers at the RAND Corporation, explained the results this way:

> In sum, then, evidence on the academic achievement of students in existing, small-scale voucher programs can be characterized as promising for low-income African Americans; showing neither harms nor benefits for other students (with a very small amount of data); and limited in its scope and breadth of applicability. (Gill et al. 2001, 90–91)

Size Still Matters

The second view of education policy suffers from the same problem as the first view: a failure to consider the size of the effects. Yes, vouchers may work, but how large is the impact? As discussed above, the best studies to date have been conducted on the private voucher programs in New York City, Dayton, Washington, and Charlottesville. Mayer and his coauthors examine the New York experiments and conclude that African American students given a voucher do approximately .20 standard deviations better on tests than African American students who are not given such an opportunity (2002, 34).[5] Howell and coauthors (2000) examine the New York, Dayton, and Washington experiments and find that African American children with a voucher increase their test scores by .085 standard deviations after one year and .165 standard deviations after two years.[6]

These effects are larger than those for increased per-pupil spending, increased teacher experience, and so on. But they are still small with respect to the massive effect of socioeconomic status on academic performance. And remember that they apply only to African American children—whites and Latinos do not appear to benefit from vouchers. Since only 31 percent of children below the poverty level are black (U.S. Census Bureau 2004), these effects apply to less than one-third of the children in question.

Filling a Hole with a Teaspoon

As in other policy contexts, both the first and second views exaggerate the effectiveness of government policies. One view argues that government policy is the *answer* to the problem of education inequalities, while the other argues that policy is the *source* of the problem. Neither conservatives nor liberals will admit the scary truth that, at present, our policy tools are inadequate to redress the achievement deficits of kids from poor families. Children whose families have low income, children who live in families headed by single women, children whose parents have little education—life digs these children into a deep educational hole before they ever get to school. Yes, we have ways to fill those holes, but our current methods are not powerful, so it is as if we are trying to fill in that hole with a teaspoon. Our efforts are simply not very effective—the playing field is certainly not level.

In one sense, the focus of the previous discussion has been theoretical: could a determined state government, using the tools of the left or the right, use education to give all children an equal start in life? As a practical matter, states don't do this—no one is actually trying to fill in the educational holes. Although state aid systems help somewhat, the major source of funding for education is the local property tax, and that gives students from wealthy districts many more resources than students from poor districts. Teachers' experience, pupil-teacher ratios, and access to books and computers are all generally better in suburban districts than in inner-city districts. For example, the National Center for Education

Statistics reports that nationwide, median household income and per pupil expenditure across school districts has a *positive* correlation of .29 (2003, 22). So the news is doubly depressing: not only are our tools for addressing inequality inadequate, but we are not truly dedicated to the task. Our current system works to deepen the "hole" of educational inequality.

Policy Implications

Should we, then, abandon the quest for educational equity? If our policy tools are not powerful, should we give up on equity and focus instead, as have many states, on "adequacy"—whatever that means?

As will be the case in our discussion of welfare, understanding the limited nature of our policy choices doesn't alter the ethical imperatives underlying education. We still recoil from the idea that a child's prospects in life would be determined by the accidents of his or her birth. And we still shudder at the idea that class differences might be perpetuated for generation after generation, especially when those class differences are strongly correlated with race and ethnicity. Such notions clash with our perception of ourselves as a free nation in which an individual's circumstances are determined by his or her own intelligence and ambition. While the statistics tell us that the road is long and difficult, our moral sense tells us that we must continue the journey.

But understanding the limitations of our policy tools has profound implications for the way we conduct education reform, and even has a bearing on wider social reforms.

Implication 1: Keep Searching

Current educational policy debates are stuck in a rut of old ideas. The literature on the effects of school characteristics is enormous and well-documented. The literature on school choice, while newer and less certain, has also been extensively debated. Too often, the states and the federal government engage in partisan controversies over policies with consequences we already know. Moreover, the record indicates that none of the policies currently under consideration are likely to have effects large enough to counteract social and economic disadvantages for poor children. Given the lack of promise for current solutions, we ought to spend more resources looking for new and innovative ones. We ought to be thinking outside the box, since what is inside the box doesn't seem to be working.

One promising line of thinking focuses on families' role in education. Since family characteristics seem to dominate educational outcomes, perhaps families can be encouraged to participate more fully in their children's education. One fresh idea has been put forward by Henry Levin and Clive Belfield (2002), who wish to see families and schools engage in a conceptual "contract" to improve children's performance.

Implication 2: Reconsider High-Stakes Testing

With the passage of the No Child Left Behind Act of 2001, President Bush made high-stakes testing the dominant reform paradigm in education. Under the law, all students must take annual tests in grades 3 through 8, with negative consequences for schools that fail to meet specified targets. But the president's action was merely the culmination of a trend, and its ultimate expression is the graduation exam: in many states, students are not allowed to graduate from high school unless they have passed a comprehensive exam. The Center on Education Policy (2003) reports that in 2003, 19 states had mandatory exit exams, and 5 more states planned to phase in tests by 2008. Already, more than half of all students in the United States are required to pass an exit exam before graduating.

The previous literature on the effect of socioeconomic status on school performance puts this testing trend in an ominous light. If the primary determinant of school performance is demographics, and if the distribution of school resources actually reinforces the inequalities among school children, graduation exams must inevitably hurt the poor and minorities. The *Atlanta Journal-Constitution* reported that, in 2004, minorities trailed whites in all fields of Georgia's high school graduation tests; the most glaring discrepancies were in English, where 96 percent of whites passed the exam while only 78 percent of Hispanics passed, and in science, where 75 percent of whites passed while only 40 percent of blacks and 36 percent of Hispanics passed.[7]

With the possibility of being denied diplomas, many poor and minority students become discouraged about their prospects to pass the test and simply drop out of school. Brian Jacob (2001), in a multivariate study comparing students in states with and without graduation exams, found that low-achieving students in states with graduation exams are 25 percent more likely to drop out than similar students in states without graduation exams, after controlling for a variety of factors affecting students, schools, and states. Amrein and Berliner (2002a) have confirmed Jacob's findings and have also found evidence that schools shunt poorly achieving students into less rigorous GED, special education, and limited English proficiency programs so that those students won't take the tests and drag down the schools' average scores. Haney (2000) found that the imposition of the Texas Assessment of Academic Skills increased dropout rates, grade 9 retention for black and Hispanic students, and classification of minority students as special education students.

Suppose that all children were required to clear a particular height in the high jump before being given a diploma. Some children, because of demographics, will be shorter and will find it harder to clear the bar. Now suppose that the shorter children, in addition their physical disadvantages, have less coaching and are given less chance to practice the high jump. Is it any wonder, then, that the shorter kids consistently fail to clear the bar?

Proponents of high-stakes testing will quickly reply that the difference between an academic test and a high jump is that the former is essential for a student's later life, while the latter is not. If students need certain skills to succeed, proponents contend, doesn't it make sense to ensure they have those skills before they leave high school? And how else would schools determine if students had the necessary skills?

The problem is that we do not know that the tests measure essential life skills, or that preparing for and passing the tests improves academic performance. Interviews with teachers reveal that "teaching to the test" is widespread, so that students are learning test-taking skills rather than fundamental skills in mathematics, reading, or writing. To ascertain whether schools teach to the test, scholars have examined the impact of testing using measures *outside* the testing instrument itself; instead of using scores on the state's graduation exams, they have examined scores on college entrance examinations (American College Testing [ACT], the Scholastic Aptitude Test [SAT], and Advanced Placement [AP] tests) and on a nationwide test given to students, called the National Assessment of Educational Progress (NAEP). They have also examined the effects of graduation exams on wider goals such as high school graduation and college enrollment. Amrein and Berliner (2002b) looked at states before and after each implemented graduation exams, and found that ACT, SAT, and AP scores actually declined. Jacob (2001) examined the results of a test given to selected students nationwide as part of the National Education Longitudinal Survey and found that graduation exams had no effect on students' 12th grade math and reading abilities. Haney (2000) found that better scores on the Texas graduation exam failed to translate into better scores on a separate college readiness test or on the SAT. Carnoy, Loeb, and Smith (2001) found that, while the Texas tests appeared to improve NAEP scores, they had little or no effect on the ultimate outcomes—high school graduation rates and the likelihood of students' attending college. According to a review of the literature by the Center on Education Policy, "the majority of studies have found no evidence that exit exams increase student learning, as measured by other indicators" (2002, 34).

Given the detrimental effects of high-stakes testing on disadvantaged children and the uncertain relationship between testing and academic achievement, we should reconsider our commitment to such testing. There is a rich irony in calling the 2001 education reform law the No Child Left Behind Act, when the testing it demands is not only unlikely to help poor children but is associated with higher dropout and retention rates for minority children.

Implication 3: Look at Welfare in a New Light

Knowing that the playing field is not level changes the way we view the competition for jobs in our economy. If, as is widely asserted, educational achievement is the key to economic success in the new economy, and if academic resources and socioeconomic background are not evenly distributed across students, then some students are continually handicapped in their pursuit of the American dream. Moreover, it will be hard for the middle class to appreciate the constraints faced by disadvantaged. Knowing that the job "game" is truly different for poor students may make it easier for taxpayers to accept that the poor need ongoing financial assistance.

For example, the fact that family background is the foremost determinant of academic achievement in primary and secondary school has profound implications for college admissions and college graduation. Students from poor families and families in which parents possess little education are likely to find getting into and graduating from college difficult. These barriers to higher education throw poor students back into the low-wage labor force. The decline of manufacturing in the United States has significantly diminished the supply of high-wage, low-education jobs, and the remaining service jobs are often characterized by frequent layoffs, unsteady hours, no health insurance, and small pay raises over time. Cast into such an unstable, unforgiving work situation, is it any wonder that low-wage workers sometimes seek help from public agencies?

Consider the situation faced by a poor single mother with a chronically ill child. Primarily because of her family background, she finds finishing high school difficult and she is unprepared for college work. She takes a service job with no health benefits and can only get help at an emergency room when her child's symptoms become acute. To give her child ongoing medical care, then, the mother may rationally decide to go on welfare and receive Medicaid (the nation's program of health insurance for the poor). If the educational playing field were level, the underprivileged woman would seem to be "milking the system" for benefits that she should be earning for her child on her own. But knowing that the playing field is not level, that there are genuine barriers and systematic disadvantages for some students, makes the disadvantaged woman seem more sympathetic, doing the best she can for her family given the circumstances dealt to her. Looking at welfare in that light may make citizens and policymakers more amenable to safety net protections for poor people.

7

The States and Competition for Economic Development

What if a state pulled out all the stops in enticing a business to locate within its borders? What happens when authorities push the limits of economic feasibility? Perhaps the largest and most controversial incentive package to date was given by the state of Alabama to Mercedes-Benz in 1993. Determined to shed its image as a sleepy southern backwater and eager to become the site of Mercedes's new SUV plant, Alabama offered these incentives:

- $92 million to buy and develop the plant site, including the construction of a $30 million worker-training center (all of the property was then sold to Mercedes for $100);
- $78 million for improvements to water, sewer, and other utilities;
- $60 million for employee-training programs;
- property tax abatements;
- sales tax abatements worth $8 million on materials used to build the plant;
- personal income tax abatements for plant workers;
- corporate income tax abatements; and
- a promise, worth $75 million, to buy 2,500 of the Mercedes SUVs for use by state authorities.[1]

The entire package was initially valued at $253 million but has since been revised upward to near $300 million.[2] Since Mercedes-Benz promised to invest only $300 million of its own money in the plant, Mercedes and Alabama can be said to be coinvestors. According to one observer, "It looks like they gave them everything but the Crimson Tide" (the University of Alabama's football team).[3]

Mercedes accepted the package and began producing SUVs in 1997. Did Alabama do the right thing? The state's early experiences with the plant were not good. Struggling to keep up the state's end of the bargain, the governor mobilized the National Guard on a "training mission" to clear the land for the site, only to be publicly criticized by a member of Congress. The governor then tried and failed to use education revenues to fund the incentive package, and the state missed a $43 million payment to Mercedes. Alabama was finally forced to borrow from its pension fund to pay for the package, at a high 9 percent rate of interest. Partly as a result of the furor over the cost of the plant, the governor was voted out of office in 1994. The most damaging figure, repeated over and over in critical press stories, was that the state ended up paying $200,000 per job at the plant—many times more than what other states have paid for economic development.[4]

However, subsequent analyses have been more positive. When the plant first opened, the company received 45,000 applications for 1,500 openings. Demand for the SUV has been strong, and the plant now runs 24 hours a day for five days a week. Workers at the plant earn $20 an hour, double the state's average wage. Mercedes made additional investments in the plant not required by the initial agreement with Alabama and hired 300 more workers than expected. Economist M. Keivan Deravi of Auburn University at Montgomery has concluded that the state has received $15 million a year from higher income, sales, and property tax due to the economic expansion.[5] In August 2000, the company announced plans for another major expansion at the plant, adding an estimated 2,000 more jobs.

The jury is still out on the Mercedes plant; to date, I know of no independent evaluation of the costs and benefits of Alabama's investment. But a substantial literature exists on the effects of such incentives in general. The analysis in this chapter is centered on three critical questions for policymakers considering similar development incentives:

- Are the incentives effective? Do they actually bring in businesses that wouldn't have located in a state or locality in the absence of those incentives?

- Are the incentives a net boon to *a state's* economy? Even if the incentives work, could a state conceivably give up so much to get a plant or sacrifice so much in alternative development activities that their net effect is negative?
- Are the incentives a net boon to *the nation's* economy? If one state manages to lure a business away from another state, the losing state could conceivably give up just as much as the winning state gains. What are the net effects of the incentives for the nation as a whole?

The "Arms Race" in Economic Development

Figures 7.1 and 7.2 illustrate the dramatic growth in economic development incentives in the last 25 years. Although policy analysts disagree somewhat about the changes in the 1990s (see Eisinger 1995), few dispute that the 1970s and 1980s saw competition between states over economic development increase dramatically. In 1977, the average state engaged in 5 of the 10 tax incentive policies listed in figure 7.1, and offered just 2 of the 9 financial incentives listed in figure 7.2; by 2004, the

Figure 7.1. Number of States Granting Tax Exemptions for Business, 1977 and 2004

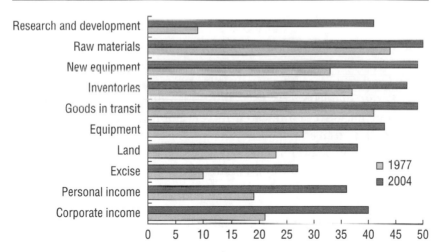

Sources: Council of State Governments (2000, 2005).

Note: Land category includes exemptions on capital improvements on land.

Figure 7.2. Number of States Granting Financial Incentives for Business, 1977 and 2004

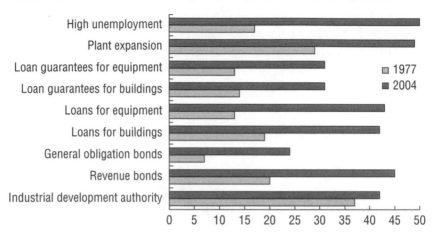

Sources: Council of State Governments (2000, 2005).

Note: The high unemployment category refers to state incentives for establishing plants in areas of high unemployment.

average state engaged in all 10 tax exemptions and 8 of the 9 financial exemptions. By 2004, a firm shopping for an industrial site could expect the vast majority of states (over two-thirds) to offer a host of incentives:

- property tax reductions on equipment, machinery, land, buildings, inventories, and raw materials;
- a personal income tax exemption for at least some workers;
- corporate income tax reductions, including accelerated depreciation, incentives for research and development, and exemptions on goods in transit;
- direct state loans for buildings, equipment, and machinery;
- tax-exempt revenue bond financing;
- the assistance of a state-sponsored industrial development authority; and
- special state incentives for locating in areas of high unemployment.

According to Bartik (1994), yearly state and local government expenditures on economic development average around $8 per capita, or about $2.2 billion in total. But this is only the most visible aspect of these programs' cost. Most spending on economic development is in the form of tax subsidies and does not show up in government budgets. Relatively little is known about the size of the subsidies, because governments do not normally gather information on revenue that they don't collect. But comprehensive studies have been performed in Michigan, New York, and Louisiana. Tax subsidies in Michigan cost about $16 per capita per year, subsidies in New York totaled $27 per capita, and subsidies in Louisiana totaled $60 per capita (Bartik 1994, 848). This would imply that tax subsidies cost the nation as a whole $4 billion to $16 billion, and total economic development costs are in the range of $6 billion to $18 billion. Despite all the attention paid to this issue, then, state and local governments spend relatively little money on economic develop ment; compare these amounts to the $279 billion spent on elementary and secondary education, or the $79 billion spent on highways, or the $71 billion spent on hospitals (U.S. Census Bureau 1999). One of the great ironies of this issue is that, as in Alabama, governors are judged and sometimes voted out of office based on one of their state's smallest expenditures.

Do Economic Development Incentives Work?

While it is becoming nearly universal for businesses to extract tax concessions and incentives from state and local governments, whether these strategies influence business locations is far from clear. Businesses have every incentive to exaggerate the importance of these incentives, to gain better incentive packages, lower their costs, and maximize their profits. Politicians, too, have an incentive to distort these incentives' importance so they can link economic expansions with their own policies. After extracting a record-breaking package of incentives for their Alabama plant, Mercedes officials later admitted that the incentives were not the deciding factor. Instead, plant officials pointed to Alabama's "low costs, quality work force, good transportation network, and quality of life."[6] Just how much difference do these incentive packages really make?

Although a variety of economic development strategies has been evaluated, most analysis has been on the effects of taxes on economic growth. Three different types of data have been used to analyze the effectiveness of economic development incentives:

- evaluations of particular development programs,
- surveys of business decisionmakers, and

- statistical studies that compare growth rates in high and low tax states, after controlling for a variety of other factors affecting growth.

Throughout the 1960s and 1970s, the wide majority of studies using any of these three methodologies came to the same conclusion: taxes appeared to make little difference to economic growth. Most studies showed that state and local taxes constituted only a tiny percentage of a typical firm's costs. The conventional wisdom was that such tiny changes in costs could not significantly affect business location, and the empirical results supported this view: tax-based development programs did not appear to work, business leaders did not identify taxes as a major factor in their location decisions, and statistical studies failed to find any significant effects of taxes on economic activity.

Beginning in the 1980s, however, some studies using new methodologies began to show small but statistically significant tax effects: these incorporated a set of control variables for previously uncontrolled confounding factors, including a state's past rates of business activity, public services, and unique characteristics (Bartik 1991, 30–33). The most thorough and influential review of this literature appeared in 1991 in a book by economist Timothy Bartik, *Who Benefits from State and Local Economic Development Policies?* Bartik summarized 71 studies done since 1979, and found that

> the most important conclusion . . . is that most recent business location studies have found some evidence of significant negative effects of state and local taxes on regional business growth. The findings of recent studies differ from those of studies in the 1950s, 1960s, and early and mid-1970s, which generally did not find statistically significant and negative effects of taxes on state and local growth. (1991, 38–39)

Though some skeptics remain (see, for example, McGuire 1992), a general consensus seems to be emerging that taxes do have significant effects on economic growth. Although the literature on public expenditures is smaller and more heterogeneous, there is also a growing consensus that public expenditures can affect economic growth (see, for example, the literature reviews by Bartik [1991, 44–48] and Fisher [1997]).

In November 1996, the Federal Reserve Bank of Boston convened a conference to bring together the best-known experts on the effectiveness of state and local economic development policies. The several literature reviews presented led conference organizers to conclude that "contrary to the conventional wisdom of the 1960s and 1970s, policies pursued by subnational governments do affect the pace of economic development within their borders."[7]

Do Incentives Boost State Economies?

Here, the empirical literature takes a surprising twist. While more and more research has shown that economic development policies work, in the sense of having an effect on location decisions, it is not at all clear that these policies yield net benefits: that is, they may not expand our budget so that we can have more of everything we want. It is as if economic development researchers were biologists, peering into more and more powerful microscopes to find a tiny, elusive, one-celled creature. Yes, as researchers have developed more and more powerful tools, they have established that economic development policies do have an effect. But the policies are not more powerful than before; it's our detection methods that have gotten stronger. Although economic development policies do have measurable effects, the impacts are generally small and limited.

Here, the gap between politicians' rhetoric and empirical results seems greatest. Ignoring all considerations of magnitude, politicians and the public cling to the simple theoretical truth that "incentives work." This logic is then used to support a general program of tax reduction to make states more "competitive," more "business friendly." Whatever must be done to keep taxes down must be accepted to keep the state properly armed in the race for jobs. By contrast, those who have studied the empirical results are markedly less dramatic in their statements. Among the experts, Bartik is one of the strongest supporters of incentives: *Who Benefits from State and Local Economic Development Policies?* was the first book to challenge the traditional academic wisdom that incentives don't work. But even Bartik is unwilling to recommend tax cuts as a general program of economic development. The results of his 1992 review of 57 empirical studies of tax cuts were published in *Economic Development Quarterly:*

> Thus, the effects of state and local taxes are significant, and large enough that they might affect some policy decisions. But it is unclear whether these tax effects are large enough that a policy of reducing state and local business taxes, adopted *solely* for the purpose of encouraging growth, would have net benefits. Such a policy might be so costly per job created that the costs of the new jobs outweigh the benefits. . . . The range from $1,906 to $10,800 in annual costs per job created is probably quite wide

from the perspective of policymakers. In many cases, perceived benefits from these new jobs are likely to lie within this range, which makes it impossible to make any firm statement about whether a policy of general business tax reductions would produce net economic benefits for the typical state or metropolitan area. (1992, 106)

Why are the experts so cautious? Recent empirical research has revealed four limitations to using tax cuts as a business development tool: (1) the effects are relatively small, (2) public services also affect growth, (3) a pure growth strategy has drawbacks, and (4) much of the benefits of growth goes to new residents.

Small Tax Effects

Almost all studies find that business activity is not sensitive to tax rates—in economists' terms, the supply curve is relatively inelastic. It takes a rather large change in tax rates to have a meaningful effect on a state's economy. In his 1992 review, Bartik concludes that the best estimate of the tax elasticity of business activity is –0.25. This means that a 10 percent reduction in tax rates should lead to a 2.5 percent long-term increase in economic activity (1992, 103).[8] Wasylenko (1997) reports similar low elasticities in his review of this literature. Phillips and Goss (1995), in a meta-analysis, report a combined elasticity of –0.35.

Public Spending and Growth

One of the reasons more recent studies have been able to detect the influence of taxes on growth is that they have carefully controlled for the available public services in each area. But this also means the interpretation of these studies changes somewhat: the numerical estimates now show the effect of cutting taxes while holding public services constant. Using Bartik's estimate above, this means that the governor who wishes to increase his state's economy by 2.5 percent must cut taxes by 10 percent while continuing to maintain the same standard of public services. In other words, the cuts must come from "fat," or inefficiency, in state and local government operations, making the governor's task much more difficult.

Alternatively, since states are required by law to balance their budgets, what if a state were to cut taxes and expenditures *at the same time?* What would be the net effect on growth? The empirical research suggests that the growth effect would be much smaller than indicated above—and might actually be negative. Fisher reviews 43 empirical studies of the effect of public services on growth and concludes that the elasticity of growth with respect to tax cuts is similar (in absolute value) to the elasticity of growth respect to public services (1997, 61). This implies that the net effect of tax and spending cuts would be close to zero. Bartik found only three studies that simultaneously tested the combined effect of lowering taxes and reducing public services. All three studies found the effects to be negative—lowering taxes and reducing services actually reduced economic growth (1992, 107).

The Costs of A Pure Growth Strategy

Could a state increase growth by cutting taxes and making *selective* cuts in services? Perhaps. Fisher finds that, of all public services, transportation, especially highways, has the greatest growth impact, followed by public safety. According to Fisher, "Of the three major public service categories reviewed here, the evidence about a relationship between economic development and spending on education is least convincing" (1997, 57). So in principle, a state could increase growth by lowering taxes and cutting education, but the magnitude of the effects might be even smaller than the relatively small elasticities given above. And such a trade-off raises serious questions about our preferences: are we willing to sacrifice, for example, our children's educations in exchange for greater economic security?

Growth and New Residents

As pointed out by Courant (1994), increased growth doesn't automatically translate into greater well-being for residents. The empirical literature is thin here, but early work by Bartik and others suggests that growth may not always be good for current residents. In a 1993 study, Bartik surveyed 19 studies and found that between 60 and 90 percent of the jobs from growth go to in-migrants or other unintended beneficiaries. Blanchard and Katz (1992) find that all of the newly created jobs in an area go to in-migrants. In a later study, Bartik (1996) found that the net fiscal impact of growth may well be negative for current residents, as new residents cost more in public services than they supply in new tax revenues.

Do Incentives Boost the National Economy?

When Alabama landed the Mercedes plant in 1993, it also meant that Alabama's rival states—principally Georgia, North Carolina, South Carolina, and Tennessee—lost the plant. Mercedes's decision to build the plant in America was independent of the incentives offered by these states; before the bidding wars began, the firm decided that high costs in Germany and high demand for SUVs in the United States dictated a U.S. location.[9] So, at least in the Mercedes case, economic development incentives appeared to provide little net gain for the nation as a whole. Traditionally, economists have concluded that most economic development activities are like the Mercedes case—one state's gain is another state's loss, with no net benefits. According to former Secretary of Labor Robert B. Reich, subsidies are "nothing but a zero-sum game. Resources are moved around; Peter is robbed to pay Paul."[10]

In the early 1990s, that pessimistic view of business incentives was challenged by *Who Benefits from State and Local Economic Development Policies?* Bartik argued that the nation as a whole might benefit from development incentives *if* the incentives were properly targeted. On an equity basis, if incentives are concentrated in low-income, high-unemployment areas, development policy might be considered a redistributive program—a way of assisting the poor without creating the work disincentives associated with welfare. On an efficiency basis, if structural unemployment exists and incentives are concentrated in areas with high unemployment, the gain to the winning jurisdiction might exceed the loss to other jurisdictions. A job lost in a booming economy may mean only that the worker turns to other, readily available positions; but a job gained in a depressed economy might be the difference between working and standing in the unemployment line.

The central empirical question, then, is whether development incentives are in fact disproportionately used by low-income, high-unemployment jurisdictions. In his 1991 book, Bartik offers some preliminary evidence that this is, in fact, the case. But subsequent research has not borne out his conjecture. Fisher and Peters use a sophisticated modeling technique to calculate how much a city or state's tax and incentive package, which they call the community's *standing incentive offer,* would save a representative firm. They then estimate the standing offers from a sample of 112 cities in 24 industrial states, concluding that,

> with regard to the overall pattern of standing offers, we find a somewhat distressing pattern. There is little reason to believe that higher unemployment states and cities provide the largest standing offers. This suggests that the antecedent condition for Bartik's argument that incentives may have net national benefits is not true: the spatial pattern of taxes and incentives in America is not likely to promote the redistribution of jobs from places of low unemployment to places of high unemployment. (1998, 26)

Similarly, in their study of cities in metropolitan Detroit, Anderson and Wassmer conclude that recent economic incentive packages were not related to income and unemployment but instead were primarily driven by the incentives offered by neighboring, competing communities: "The information in this book clearly shows that, when communities are left to their own devices, local economic development incentives are increasingly offered by places that do not fit the 'high unemployment and fiscally blighted' characterization" (2000, 174).

In a later paper, Bartik (1992) supplies a final discouraging note on the distributional effect of financial incentives. We have assumed until now that businesses are equally tax sensitive in all locations—that the effects of tax cuts and other economic incentives are equal throughout the country. This is obviously a restrictive assumption. A review of the empirical literature finds that outlying suburbs are most likely to reap benefits from economic development incentives, while central cities are least likely to find these incentives effective. Apparently, then, the most needy places will find economic development incentives the least helpful.

Compared to the evidence on the effects of taxes on business locations, we are less certain of the distributional impact of economic development incentives. Nevertheless, the best available information offers no assurance that the distribution of these incentives is good for poor people or for the national economy.

What about "New Wave" Industrial Development Activity?

If the conservative answer to economic development is tax cuts, the liberal answer is a series of government programs designed to provide firms, especially small start-ups, with services and encouragement. According to Bartik, these "new wave" economic development policies include

- loans and loan guarantees;
- education and information for small business entrepreneurs, including small business development centers, entrepreneurial-training programs, and community college classes in starting a business;
- programs for research in high technology, including applied research grants, research-oriented industrial parks, and technology transfer programs from universities; and
- export assistance, including export financing, trade missions, and export information and expertise (1991, 4).

What do we know about these programs' effectiveness? As it turns out, relatively little. While several studies have suggested these programs are helpful, the evidence is weak. Most of these studies use data supplied by surveys that simply ask users whether they found the services helpful and to what degree. There are at least three major problems with this approach. First, respondents have an incentive to overemphasize the programs' importance to ensure their continuation. Second, the surveys may reveal perceived effects on *profitability,* but this is not the same as identifying effects on *firm behavior.* The programs may fatten a firm's bottom line, but does that mean it will stay in an area, expand its operations, or hire more employees? Since owners may not keep their money within the state where their firms are located, simply enhancing the returns to owners may not be the best policy objective. Third, sorting out the factors contributing to a firm's success is often a complex business. Did the firm succeed because of a strong economy, competent executives, diligent workers, or wise government policy, or because of some combination of all of these factors? Business leaders preoccupied with day-to-day management might not be able to provide more than unsystematic, impressionistic answers.

The honest answer, then, is that we simply don't know whether these "new wave" economic development programs work or not. Until more studies can be done using high-quality controls for confounding factors, the jury is still out.

Conclusions: The "Third View" of Economic Development Policy

To date, the literature on the effects of economic development policies supports two conclusions: (1) in some circumstances, economic development policies can work, in the sense of altering business location and employment decisions; however, (2) none of the current policies have been shown to work well enough to pay for themselves in increased state tax revenues from higher economic activity. And there is no convincing evidence that these policies benefit the nation's economy.

In terms of the Alabama Mercedes case study that began this chapter, no comprehensive accounting of costs and benefits has been completed, and the case is not necessarily typical of most economic development policies. But the existing literature suggests that tax cuts and development subsidies probably did help Alabama attract the Mercedes plant. Unfortunately, the effects of the incentive package were not large enough to spare Alabama some hard choices. A state can help attract a firm like Mercedes with tax cuts and development subsidies, but revenues for other programs like education, welfare, and health care are likely to decrease. Among contemporary scholars, Bartik holds a relatively favorable view of the benefits of economic development subsidies; but after a review of the relevant literature, even he concludes that "contrary to some claims, tax and financial incentives are *not* a free lunch for a state or metropolitan area. These programs do not create enough jobs and new tax revenue that the programs have little or no net cost" (1994, 854).

The debate between liberals and conservatives on economic development typically centers on the right method to jump start a state's economy. The implicit assumption is that a fix is available—if only we can find it. But the empirical literature suggests that there is currently no fix, just a series of trade-offs, a set of choices about the kind of society we want to live in. Taxes and spending do have behavioral effects on firms, but the effects are not large enough to sweep aside redistributional, investment, and service considerations for state policy. Yes, Alabama may be able to attract an auto plant by offering large tax cuts and development incentives, and providing high-wage jobs is a legitimate policy goal. However, educating Alabama's children is also a legitimate goal, as is providing health care for Alabama's poor. The real question is, how much education and health care are Alabama willing to give up to get the additional jobs? Would a society with higher wages but fewer formally educated workers be preferable to the status quo? Would a society with higher wages but less health care for the needy be better than what we have now?

Justice Louis Brandeis once wrote that "the states are the laboratories of democracy." States should be allowed to experiment with new economic development policies, some of which may turn out to be more powerful than our current tools. And we need more research on some currently available tools, such as "new wave" development policies. But at present, our economic development tools represent yet another example of the economists' dictum that "there's no such thing as a free lunch." Productive public discussions about economic development must go beyond strictly financial considerations and must combine realistic, empirically based calculations of the trade-offs confronting us with open discussions about our values as a society.

8

What Did Your Congressman Learn in School?

When I was in graduate school, our microeconomic theory instructor (the most famous professor in the school) always said that his course had no great themes or descriptive content. Instead, the course was a collection of tools for use in later projects. His message stuck with me, and later when I taught undergraduate statistics for public policy majors, I told my students the same thing. I even brought a tool belt to class, complete with hammer, screwdrivers, and pencils, to dramatize the point.

But my experiences with students have also taught me to ask an important related question. If some courses are simply tool courses, when do students learn the realities of the world around them? When do they get the empirical content they need? If theory classes help students learn to master the mechanics of graphs and equations, when do they learn about crucial economic parameters? When do they get information about individual, market, and macroeconomic responses to government activities? When do students get answers to questions like the ones below?

- How sensitive are workers to their wages—are they willing to work much more if their wages increase by, say, a dollar? This question is crucial to both tax policy and welfare policy.
- How sensitive is individual saving to tax rates? This question is important for tax policy and long-term economic growth.

- How sensitive is the housing supply to changes in the rate of return on housing? This question is central to the issues of the appropriate property tax and the desirability (or undesirability) of rent control.
- How much inefficiency do tariffs and quotas on imported goods create? This question is fundamental in discussions of trade policy.

No doubt the answers to these questions are controversial. Economists have a deserved reputation for disagreeing with each other; George Bernard Shaw said, "if all economists were laid end to end, they would not reach a conclusion." But don't students deserve to learn the best available information on these questions? Even if some of these parameters cannot be pinned down to their precise values, can't some values be dismissed as extremely unlikely? In other words, can't we give students a likely range for the relevant parameters? The great danger is that, if we don't supply our students with any empirical evidence, they will "fill in the blanks" with values borne of intuition and ideology. Conservatives, for example, are free to assume that the supplies of labor, savings, and housing are all extremely responsive to the changes in their respective prices, making government interference in the economy undesirable. Liberals, on the other hand, are free to assume that all of these factors are extremely unresponsive to price, making government interference more acceptable.

In this chapter, I examine the economic and statistical education of members of Congress. Could a lack of empirical grounding contribute to the overestimated effects of government policies described in this book?[1]

The Educational Background of Congress

Figures 8.1 and 8.2 illustrate the educational preparation of members of Congress, focusing on the highest degree attained. As the figures show, the most common training is a B.A. or B.S. followed by a law degree. Over half the members of the Senate have law degrees (L.L.B. or J.D.), as do more than one-third of the members of the House. Congress does not keep reliable records on its members' undergraduate majors, but according to the American Economic Association, 40 percent of all undergraduates in four-year colleges and universities take at least one economics course (Siegfried 2000). Given senators' and representatives' public pol-

Figure 8.1. Highest Degree Received by U.S. Senators, 107th Congress, 2nd Session

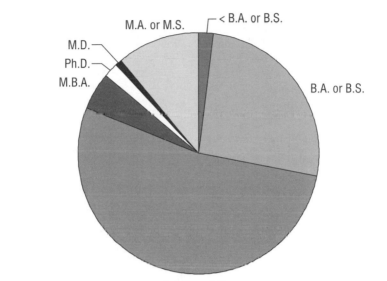

Sources: Author's calculations from congressmembers' web sites and Congressional Quarterly (2002).

Notes: M.A. or M.S. also includes M.S.W., M.P.A., M.P.P, M. Div., D.V.M., M.L.S., M.Ed., and M.S.I.A. Several members of Congress (5 in the Senate, 21 in the House) held multiple master's degrees but no Ph.D., making assignment of "highest" degree somewhat difficult. Based on the time typically required for each program, the M.D. degree was ranked highest, followed by L.L.B. or J.D., other master's, and finally, M.B.A. Given the small number of these cases, the conclusions from these figures would not be substantially altered by an alternative set of rankings.

icy interests, even more than 40 percent of them have likely taken some economics during their undergraduate careers.

Searching for Empirical Content in the Economics Curriculum

In an effort to find out how much economics students learn about real phenomena, I examined the undergraduate curricula at six top departments of economics: Princeton, Harvard, MIT, Northwestern, Yale, and

Figure 8.2. Highest Degree Received by U.S. Congressional
Representatives, 107th Congress, 2nd Session

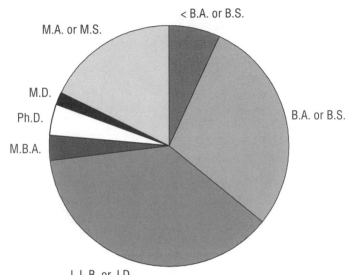

Sources: Author's calculations from congressmembers' web sites and Congressional Quarterly
(2002).

Notes: M.A. or M.S. also includes M.S.W., M.P.A., M.P.P, M. Div., D.V.M., M.L.S., M.Ed., and
M.S.I.A. Several members of Congress (5 in the Senate, 21 in the House) held multiple master's
degrees but no Ph.D., making assignment of "highest" degree somewhat difficult. Based on the
time typically required for each program, the M.D. degree was ranked highest, followed by L.L.B.
or J.D., other master's, and finally, M.B.A. Given the small number of these cases, the conclusions
from these figures would not be substantially altered by an alternative set of rankings.

Stanford. These schools were chosen because they were the only ones to
appear in the top 10 of three national rankings of economics departments:
those of *US News and World Report*,[2] the National Research Council
(Goldberger, Maher, and Flattau 1995), and Dusansky and Vernon
(1998).[3] In what follows, I divide the economics curriculum into three
parts: principles courses, core courses, and electives.

Principles Courses

Every department surveyed provided a one- or two-semester introductory principles course. All of the departments required principles

before further study in economics. The content of these courses is extremely important, because most students' economic education ends with principles.

To find out what is taught in these principles courses, I examined the universities' web sites and e-mailed their professors to ask which textbooks they used. In these six schools, only five textbooks were used by more than one professor in the 2001–2002 school year:

- William J. Baumol and Alan S. Blinder, *Economics: Principles and Policy,* 8th edition (Mason, Ohio: South-Western Publishing, 1999);
- Karl E. Case and Ray C. Fair, *Principles of Economics,* 6th edition (Upper Saddle River, New Jersey: Prentice Hall, 2001);
- N. Gregory Mankiw, *Principles of Economics,* 2nd edition (Fort Worth, Texas: Harcourt College Publishers, 2001);
- Paul A. Samuelson and William D. Nordhaus, *Economics,* 17th edition (Boston, Massachusetts: McGraw-Hill Irwin, 2001); and
- John B. Taylor, *Economics,* 3rd edition (Boston, Massachusetts: Houghton Mifflin Co., 2001).

These texts reveal that principles courses are primarily about tools, with the emphasis on mastering certain theoretical models, usually represented by graphs. Typically, the books cover topics such as the following:

- the supply and demand model of market equilibrium,
- the cost-structure model of a competitive firm and its implications for firm behavior,
- the graphical model of output and price decisions for a monopolist, and
- the aggregate demand–aggregate supply model of a macro economy.

All of these are theoretical concepts built up from first principles, based on assumptions about technology and the pure logic of utility maximization. No empirical data are used in formulating them.

Often, the textbooks do include some applied chapters addressing topics such as labor markets, income inequality, environmental problems, and the tax system. These chapters often contain some empirical material, although this is usually basic institutional and descriptive data (such as the structure of the income tax and the extent of poverty in the

United States) rather than results of studies about the size of relevant parameters.

To assess how much empirical material the textbooks contain, I cataloged their ubiquitous boxes, charts, and other graphical material. Each book contained from 400 to 612 of these graphics boxes, with the breakdown of material given in figure 8.3.

As you can see, the majority of graphic material (55 percent) is used to illustrate, reinforce, and explain theoretical material. Only 18 percent of the boxes used in text contain figures and tables with real-world data; another 2 percent of boxes are sidelights containing figures and tables with empirical data. All told, then, only one in five graphics contains real data.

Moreover, even these weak numbers probably overstate the empirical content of principles textbooks for two reasons. First, the most popular text, Mankiw's *Principles of Economics,* also contains the least

Figure 8.3. Types of Illustration in Economics Principles Texts

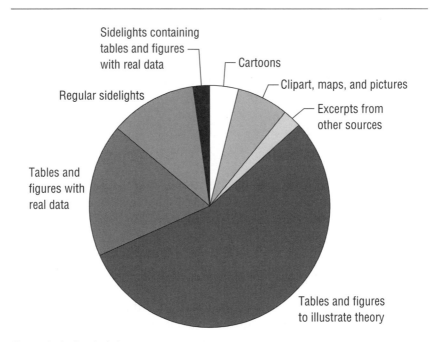

Source: Author's calculations.

Note: Author's calculations are based on a selection of five widely used textbooks. See text for details.

empirical material. Since the figure above used straight (rather than sales-weighted) averages, these numbers probably represent an overestimate. Second, as discussed above, much of the empirical content is contained in a few "applied" chapters on topics such as labor, the environment, and taxation. Instructors are not compelled to cover everything in the textbook, and if time is short they are likely to omit one or more of these applied chapters rather than the book's theoretical core.

Overall, it seems unlikely that students learn much empirical material in the principles courses, and we must look elsewhere in the curriculum for this material.

Core Courses

For the relatively few students that do go beyond principles, all of the schools required a series of core courses: microeconomic theory, macroeconomic theory, and one or two semesters of statistics and econometrics. Not surprisingly, micro theory and macro theory courses contain almost no empirical content. They are intended to help the student master the mechanics of certain models, not to teach them the properties of real economies. Examples and applications in these courses do sometimes incorporate real data. But here the data serve the theory, not the other way around. The instructor and textbook author simply pick examples that seem particularly apt to the theory at hand and that might spark students' interest. So the empirical content included is necessarily random and shallow. The courses make little attempt to provide students with a survey of a body of empirical data.

What may be surprising, however—at least if you are not an economist—is that the statistics and econometrics courses are also theoretical tools courses. While the *subject* of these courses is by definition empirical, their *approach* is theoretical. Students master the theories of probability, descriptive statistics, hypothesis testing, regression, and so forth. Again, examples are used, but they provide only limited, scattershot empirical content. Students leave these courses knowing the probability of drawing six red cards and two black cards out of a standard deck but remaining ignorant about the elasticity of labor supply or the effect of taxation on saving. Here is a typical econometrics course description from one of the schools:

An introduction to multiple regression techniques with focus on economic applications. Discusses extensions to discrete response, panel data, and time series models, as well as issues such as omitted variables, missing data, sample selection, randomized and natural experiments, and instrumental variables. Aims to provide students with an understanding of and ability to apply econometric and statistical methods using computer packages.[4]

Electives

If principles and core courses don't provide much empirical content, then we must look for it in the electives. But depending on electives raises at least three problems:

1. Many electives are, in fact, theoretical, with course titles such as Economics of Discontinuous Change, Economic Theory of Environment and Natural Resources, Introduction to Game Theory, Advanced Contract Theory, and Nonlinear Econometric Analysis. Even traditional electives, like health economics or urban economics, can be taught from a theoretical orientation, concentrating on advances in modeling techniques rather than the empirical studies available. With few exceptions, instructors are free to teach the courses as theoretically as they wish.

2. Only a minority of electives require statistics or econometrics. This means that, in most cases, the instructor cannot use the empirical tools taught in the core courses. Instructors could provide empirical information about economic factors, but without using statistics and econometrics they cannot put that information into appropriate context. Most importantly, without a statistics prerequisite, the instructor will find it difficult to convey the strength of the data presented. Did the data come from large-scale experiments or were they the result of a few isolated case studies? Were the relevant confounding factors controlled for or were they left free to conflate the results? Were the appropriate methodological tools used to analyze the data? Without the appropriate statistical cautions, students often react to empirical data in one of two inappropriate ways: either taking the instructor's assertions as gospel, so that the student rejects any subsequent information that conflicts with the instructor's opinions, or adopting the attitude that "you can prove anything by manipulating the statistics," which leaves him or her free to form opinions based on intuition, ideology, or prejudice.

3. By the very nature of electives, students graduate with incomplete and nonstandardized information rather than a core of empirical

knowledge. If students later confront public policy issues outside the scope of their electives, they will be empirically unprepared. Furthermore, the scattershot approach makes it difficult for students to assess issues that cut across more than one field.

Statistical Training in Law School

Does legal education remedy these deficiencies in the economics curriculum? What statistical education do future congressional representatives get in law school? Usually, none at all.

I investigated the 2001–2002 catalogs from six of the top U.S. law schools: Columbia, Harvard, Michigan, New York University, the University of California at Berkeley, and Yale.[5] None of the schools required any statistical training. Three of the schools (NYU, UC Berkeley, and Yale) offered no electives covering statistics. Harvard and Columbia offered full-semester elective courses on statistics for lawyers, while Michigan offered a course on analytical methods that provided a few weeks of instruction in statistics. But the enrollment in these optional courses was terribly small; on average, only 6 percent of the students in the three schools took a statistics course. All together, then, our best guess is that just 3 percent of the students in these six top law schools were exposed to statistical training during law school.

This lack of statistical sophistication is also reflected in the journals that fuel law professors' lectures. A recent review of hundreds of law journal articles by two distinguished political science professors concluded that "the current state of empirical legal scholarship is deeply flawed . . . We find that serious problems of inference and methodology abound everywhere we find empirical research in the law reviews and in articles written by members of the legal community" (Epstein and King 2002, 6 and 15). The authors go on to sharply contrast legal education with graduate education in other fields: "While a Ph.D. is taught to subject his or her favored hypothesis to every conceivable test and data source, seeking out all possible evidence against his or her theory, an attorney is taught to amass all the evidence for his or her hypothesis and distract attention from anything that might be seen as contradictory information" (Epstein and King 2002, 9). No wonder lawmakers have difficulty objectively weighing the evidence for their positions.

Of course, as one law school professor pointed out to me, there are other ways in which law students might be exposed to statistics. Some students come to law school with prior training in statistics as undergraduates; some students pursue joint degrees in fields such as public administration or public policy, which require statistics; some law courses, particularly those in evidence and law and economics, include a bit of statistical material; and some students take elective courses outside their law schools involving statistics.

So the number of "statistically aware" law students is probably higher than 3 percent. But even the most optimistic observers admit that few students get statistical training in these other ways, and the training is certainly uneven and haphazard. If, as I suggest, a knowledge of statistics is a fundamental skill, no educational reformer would suggest that law students learn it in such a random and unpredictable fashion. Only a tiny minority of law students receive the appropriate statistical training necessary to evaluate the information in policy debates.

Conclusion: Education and Congressional Decisions

Members of Congress have remarkably little empirical foundation for the policy decisions they must make. They may well have taken a course in principles of economics, but these courses contain little empirical information, usually of a descriptive nature. A small percentage of them majored in economics,[6] but their core courses used empirical data only as examples to illustrate the theory they were learning. Their elective courses may have provided a small amount of empirical material, but it was probably incomplete and not placed in appropriate statistical context. Only a tiny percentage of representatives received any statistical training in law school. It is not surprising, then, that these men and women spend little time objectively evaluating the evidence behind policy choices—they have not been trained to do so.

This implies that, when a member of Congress confronts a policy question, he or she is unlikely to know the sizes of the relevant parameters. Further, when presented with statistical data from researchers, congressional staff, the press, or interest groups, he or she is not likely to be prepared to evaluate them against the hierarchy of statistical information (figure 2.1). Worse, he or she may not be aware that statistical evaluation of policy claims is even possible. Policy decisions are thus decided on anything but empirical grounds. Statisticians warn against inferring causality from simple associations, so I will not argue that senators' and representatives' education "causes" the exaggerated beliefs about government policy documented in this book. However, their education certainly does little to counteract those exaggerations.

9

Welfare without Illusions

Whatever else they disagreed on, President Clinton and Republican leaders in Congress agreed on one thing in 1996: the old welfare system had to go. Depending on whom you talked to, the old system kept people in poverty by failing to educate or train them, by stigmatizing them, by fostering racial and class-based stereotypes, by discouraging work, by encouraging out-of-wedlock births, or by contributing to "a culture of dependence." Although the president vetoed two welfare reform measures before he signed the Personal Responsibility and Work Opportunity Reconciliation Act in August 1996, his opposition was to the *methods* used by Congress, not to the principle of overhauling welfare. Indeed, he had campaigned in 1992 to "end welfare as we know it," a goal eagerly embraced by the public. And congressional Republicans, longtime opponents of the welfare system, wanted to seize the moment to make truly revolutionary changes.

Today, federal and state politicians are still rushing to claim credit for the 1996 reforms. The welfare rolls have decreased dramatically across every region of the country. States have been released to make sweeping changes and many have responded eagerly, enacting bold and innovative programs. Success stories from now-employed former welfare recipients are told and retold.

This chapter reviews what we know about welfare and poverty, examining how the welfare debate might change if our limited ability to end poverty were fully recognized.

The Old and New Welfare Systems

For some recipients, the old and new welfare systems are more similar than the conventional wisdom might suggest. For aged, blind, and disabled poor people, the Supplemental Security Income (SSI) system continues relatively unchanged, although eligibility rules have been tightened. Benefits are primarily determined by the federal government (although some states choose to supplement these benefits) and are indexed for inflation. Eligibility standards are also nationally determined. And the federal Food Stamp program continues to help many poor people, although eligibility has been tightened and benefits have been trimmed.

But for single mothers receiving welfare, the world has changed dramatically. Under the old system, they were covered by a program called Aid to Families with Dependent Children (AFDC). Under AFDC, the states set eligibility and benefits, and assistance had no time limits. The federal government contributed between 50 and 78 percent of each state's AFDC program, depending inversely on the state's per capita income. The Department of Health and Human Services (HHS) published books of regulations for the states to follow and backed up its demands with a threat to withdraw financial support.

All that changed in 1996. Under the new system, AFDC is now replaced by Temporary Assistance for Needy Families (TANF). States still set eligibility and benefits, but many of the federal regulations are gone. The new system is flexible on *means* but rigid on *goals*. Within broad limits, states are free to organize their TANF programs any way they wish. But the federal government still gives states specific targets for recipients' employment, and failure to meet those targets can cost states billions of aid dollars.

The program's relationship with individuals has changed, too. TANF emphasizes *temporary* assistance. Individuals can receive no more than two years of assistance at any time without gaining employment, with a lifetime limit of five years of assistance. Finally, TANF is financed differently. Rather than paying a percentage of the welfare program's cost, the federal government gives block grants that are (within limits) independent of program spending.

The Levers of the Left: Government as a Catalyst for Change

Government programs meant to improve the plight of the poor have been under vigorous attack for almost 30 years. The Reagan administration used stories of failed government programs so effectively that they became a virtual cliché. The rejection of governmental activism has been so complete that it is curious to find its resurgence at the state level. Ignoring the lessons of the federal experience, states are dashing to find the "magic bullet" that magically transforms welfare recipients into middle-class wage earners. Some have put their faith in industry-specific job-training programs. Others have emphasized "job clubs," which teach welfare recipients how to prepare a resumé, how to behave in an interview, and how to search for work. Still others have concentrated on alleviating barriers to work by providing transportation, day care, or health care.

One of the most important behavioral questions is whether government programs help welfare recipients train for and obtain good jobs. Thankfully, this subject has been thoroughly examined before. In the 1960s, the federal government implemented the Work Incentive Program to provide training and job-search assistance for welfare recipients; in 1988, the government instituted Job Opportunities and Basic Skills Training for the same purposes. These programs allowed states flexibility similar to the current welfare reform provisions— some states provided job-search training and job-placement information, some provided counseling and group discussions of work problems and attitudes, some provided education, and some provided public sector employment. And the programs have been closely monitored and evaluated, so we now have a good idea of their effects.

The general consensus among those who have studied this literature is that these programs work, in the sense of increasing employment and earnings among the target population. For many of the women in these studies, who would have eventually returned to work even without assistance, the programs accelerated their return to the labor force. But there are three very large caveats to remember:

1. *The gains in earnings are small.* Rebecca Blank of the Brookings Institution concludes that most programs increased earnings by $150 to $600 *per year* (1997, 176). Such small gains, while helpful, are not enough to bring these women out of poverty and are not enough to "solve" the welfare problem.

2. *The gains in earnings were almost all due to increased work hours,* not to higher wages (Blank 1997, 176).

3. *These small earnings gains must be seen in the context of painfully low wages.* The jobs available to welfare recipients, who typically have little education and job experience, are usually minimum-wage positions that don't raise their standard of living. In fact, working often makes the former recipient worse off than under welfare. Kathryn Edin and Laura Lein (1997) did in-depth personal interviews with 379 low-income single mothers in Boston, Charleston, Chicago, and San Antonio in the early 1990s, piecing together their family budgets. Of those women, 165 worked more or less full-time and 214 depended on welfare (although many of these women on welfare also had part-time jobs). Surprisingly, the working women suffered higher degrees of material hardship than the welfare recipients, experiencing food shortages, hunger, and utility shutoffs more frequently than the welfare recipients. Even though the working mothers earned more than the welfare recipients, they had much higher costs for child care, clothing, health care, housing, and transportation, and their income was much more uncertain because they were subject to layoffs and seasonal reductions in work hours.

Similar discouraging results have been found with other programs affecting the poor. Programs aimed at reducing teen pregnancy have been disappointing, as have been job-training programs for men and programs focused on high school dropouts (Blank 1997, 176–83).

For many on the left, these results just demonstrate that we haven't gone far enough, that we haven't invested enough in the poor. What about the things we *haven't* tried? they ask. One of the most common prescriptions from the left is for education. After reviewing the plight of hundreds of low-income mothers, Edin and Lein conclude that the only answer for these women is a two-year degree from a technical school or community college, which would enable them to earn a living wage of $8 to $10 an hour (1997, 232–35). Because this approach has never been tried on any large scale, the argument is difficult to evaluate empirically. We have little data from which to make projections. But there are three large problems with this idea:

1. *Such an educational program would be extremely expensive,* compared with the current welfare program. Welfare families now receive average cash benefits of less than $4,000 per year.[1] A year of community

college costs $7,500 on average,[2] and full-time child care costs another $4,500.[3] Since a welfare recipient would probably need all three of these to pursue higher education (cash assistance, education, and child care), the total cost could equal $16,000 —*quadruple* current welfare costs. And for fairness reasons, these benefits would have to be offered not only to welfare recipients but to low-income working families, raising the costs even further. If we provide welfare recipients with education that puts them above the poverty level, we could not deny similar benefits to anyone below it. Currently, only about one-third of those below the poverty level receive cash assistance. This means that, to bring welfare recipients out of poverty and to be fair to all, another *tripling* of expenditures would be required.

2. *Many welfare recipients will not be able to benefit from education.* Because of stricter eligibility requirements for SSI, a large number of poor people with physical, psychological, or mental impairments find themselves instead on TANF. Many of these recipients will be unable to handle college work or even a full-time job. And of course, some recipients have drug and alcohol problems that would prevent them from succeeding in a two-year program. Some of these difficulties can be remedied by psychological counseling, physical therapy, work retraining, and drug rehabilitation—but again, only at much higher expense than the current program.

3. *Extrapolating from a few individuals or small programs can lead to a "fallacy of composition."* What works for one individual may not work for the millions on welfare. If, as suggested by Edin and Lein, all welfare recipients were to train for $8 to $10 an hour jobs in "pharmaceutical, dental, and medical technology and in accounting, business, and cosmetology" (1997, 82), would there be enough jobs in those fields to go around? If there were enough jobs, what would happen to their wages? If, as many liberals contend, the welfare problem is primarily a labor-market problem caused by our economy's failure to generate enough high-wage, low-skill jobs, can we solve that problem without attacking the fundamentals of the economy?

All of this suggests that, within the current political constraints on spending, government activism cannot do much. Given our current political climate and current understanding of poverty, the liberal levers cannot solve the welfare problem.

The Levers of the Right: Government as Disease Agent

Given the extent to which the government activism of the 1960s has been so widely discredited, the position of conservatives on welfare reform has been ironic, for they have constructed a vision of poverty parallel to that of liberals. For many conservatives, government continues to be a powerful and pervasive influence on the lives of the poor, and therefore pulling government-policy levers remains the key to changing their behavior and eliminating poverty. The difference is that for conservatives, the levers work backward: high rates of government assistance are associated with reduced work effort, more out-of-wedlock births, and a larger number of single-parent families.

The poor, conservatives argue, are affected because government programs give inappropriate incentives. Give a poor person welfare benefits, and they will have an incentive to work less. If the benefits depend upon having children, the poor will have an incentive to have more children. If the benefits also depend upon remaining single, then the poor will have an incentive not to marry. According to conservatives, these incentives have led to the destruction of the social fabric, leading to more poverty (see, for example, Murray 1984). The solution to all these problems is therefore simple: reduce welfare, reduce its incentives for inappropriate behavior, and the problems will disappear.

The problem with the conservative view is that, while it pays careful attention to economic theory, it ignores the empirical realities, the real-world magnitudes, of its effects. Simplistic theories often exclude important factors from the models. When those additional factors are included in the picture, we typically find that government policy has little or no adverse effect on the behavior of the poor.

Perhaps the hottest of the hot-button issues in welfare is the potential effect of welfare on out-of-wedlock births. Since we typically give public assistance to one-parent but not two-parent families, and we give little to childless couples and singles without disabilities, doesn't welfare give the poor an incentive to have children they can't afford? Recent statistics seem to back this up: just 5.3 percent of all births were to unmarried women in 1960, but this rose to 27.7 percent by 1990. The trends are particularly alarming for teenage and African American women (Martin et al. 2007).

But this simple theoretical story has numerous empirical holes. First of all, welfare benefits are not indexed for inflation and have declined substantially in real terms in the last 30 years. Why would poor women have more babies for less money? Second, as pointed out by Rebecca Blank and several other writers, the birth rate among unmarried women has risen in all classes of society, not just poor people (Blank 1997, 149). And it has risen in all industrialized societies, not just the United States. If American welfare is the culprit by giving incentives to poor single mothers, how does it influence middle-class women? And how does it influence women in other countries, many of which do not limit aid to single-parent families? Something larger, something more powerful than welfare, must be at work.

Numerous studies have examined the role of welfare on recipients' birth rates, after controlling for the many other factors affecting a woman's decision to have children. The general consensus is that welfare has little or no effect on a woman's decision to have a child. As noted in chapter 2, Robert Moffitt (1992), a professor of economics at Johns Hopkins University and a well-known expert on welfare, has concluded from the extensive empirical literature on this question that the welfare system has had little effect on the number of female-headed families in the United States.

An additional highly charged issue is the effect of welfare on work incentives. The conservative line is that welfare, by giving disincentives to work, lures low-income women away from work and undermines the possibility of climbing the economic ladder. And indeed, a massive number of studies do suggest that the old welfare system, which reduced welfare benefits dollar-for-dollar with increased earnings, did cause welfare recipients to work less. But the effects are much smaller than the rhetoric of the right would suggest.

Our best guess is that if the old welfare system had been completely eliminated, the former recipients would have worked about *five hours* more per week (Moffitt 1992, 16). This means that welfare does replace work earnings, but only to a small degree. Most importantly, the evidence suggests that if welfare were eliminated, the typical single-parent family of recipients would not earn enough to pull themselves above the poverty level (Moffitt 1992, 16). In other words, the evidence suggests that people are not poor because they receive welfare; rather, they receive welfare because they are poor.

Effects of the 1996 Act: It's the Economy, Stupid!

The recent figures on welfare rolls are quite startling. Nationwide, the welfare caseload declined by an incredible 59 percent from 1994 to 2002 (Besharov 2003, 6). Most scholars agree that the largest contributor to this remarkable result was the strong economy of the late 1990s:

> Looking across all the studies, and discounting the weakest ones, the most reasonable conclusion is that, although welfare reform was an important factor in reducing caseloads (accounting for 25 to 35 percent of the decline), the economy was probably more important (35 to 45 percent of the decline) and expanded aid to low-income, working families (primarily through the Earned Income Tax Credit, or EITC) was almost as important as welfare reform (20 to 30 percent). (Besharov 2003, 9)

Earlier studies also reached the conclusion that the economy has significant effects on welfare caseloads (For a review, see Blank 2002). Before the 1996 reforms, states were able to accomplish many of the same goals they are now pursuing (tightening eligibility requirements and strengthening work requirements) through individually requested "waivers" from the Department of Health and Human Services. However, in a widely cited Council of Economic Advisers (CEA) report, the Clinton administration concluded that economic improvement was the largest single cause of the decline in states' average welfare caseload from 1993 to 1996, responsible for 44 percent of the reductions (Council of Economic Advisers 1997). About one-third of the drop in the welfare rolls was attributable to the waivers.

But the most surprising finding from the CEA report was that a good part of the decline was caused by a "threat effect," not by any improvement in the alternatives available to the poor. In other words, the mere threat of a waiver that would increase the recipients' work requirements will reduce the caseload—even before the work requirement takes effect. According to the CEA, a waiver requirement that takes effect one year from now will reduce the *current* welfare rolls by 6 percent. The CEA also found that caseloads declined the most in states with the toughest sanctions (Council of Economic Advisers 1999). Put simply, it is possible to scare welfare recipients off the rolls, although there is no evidence that doing so improves recipients' lives.

Where Are They All Going?

The obvious question to ask right now is, where are all of those leaving the welfare rolls going? Are they getting good jobs that provide a living wage and a chance for advancement, or do they end up unemployed and on the streets? In short, has the 1996 reform act made them better off? Surprisingly, the 1996 act required no comprehensive assessment of those leaving welfare. To a remarkable degree, this radical surgery on the welfare system has been performed without formal monitoring of the patient's vital signs.

However, in a piecemeal and uncoordinated fashion, numerous states have independently compiled information about former welfare recipients. Unfortunately, these studies have focused primarily on their work behavior, with little information on their well-being.[4] However, large studies are also being compiled by the RAND Corporation, the Urban Institute, Manpower Demonstration Research Corporation, and others. Various outcomes measures have been used: incomes, consumption, measures of hardship (such as whether the family has had their utilities cut off or run out of food), and children's educational achievements and social adjustment. And various comparison groups have been employed:

- In some early studies under the old welfare waiver programs, welfare recipients were randomly assigned to "treatment" and "control" groups.
- Welfare recipients under the current system have been compared to previous welfare recipients under the old system.
- "Welfare leaver" studies have compared the well-being of those who have left welfare with their well-being while on welfare.
- Current single mothers have been compared with the current married poor (since the latter are largely unaffected by welfare reform).
- Those now on welfare have been compared with those who are no longer on welfare.

This diverse collection of studies does support three general conclusions. *First, welfare reform, for all its hype, has had surprisingly little effect—good or bad—on the well-being of the poor.* For the most part, the estimated effects are small and the research results are contradictory, suggesting no pattern one way or the other.

- *Income and economic hardships.* Mayer and Sullivan summarized more than a dozen welfare leaver studies and concluded that "family incomes of leavers tend to be lower or similar to their combined earnings and benefits before exit (leaving welfare)," and "there is some evidence that former welfare recipients are more likely to experience hardships such as difficulty providing food, paying utilities, or paying rent" (2001, 6). On the other hand, Danziger and his coauthors (2002) compared current welfare recipients with former welfare recipients in the late 1990s and concluded that the working group had higher income than those receiving welfare. However, the two groups experienced similar material hardship.
- *Marriage and children.* Fein and his coauthors, in their review of numerous welfare reform demonstration programs, reported that "studies of single parents have found small, mixed impacts on marriage . . . So far, most evaluations have not found impacts on childbearing" (2002, 5–6). One recent study (Kaestner, Korenman, and O'Neill 2003) concluded that teenagers after welfare reform were less fertile and married less often than teenagers before welfare reform, but cautioned that more research is necessary to say whether welfare reform caused the changes.
- *Effects on young children.* Chase-Lansdale and coauthors, in an influential 2003 article in *Science* magazine, studied 2,402 low-income families and found little difference in young children's educational achievement or social adjustment after leaving welfare.[5] Likewise, Grogger, Karoly, and Klerman (2002), in a synthesis of 67 studies, found that work requirements had no strong impacts on grade school children.
- *Effects on adolescents.* Trzcinski and Brandell (2001) used two national surveys of families to examine the effects of welfare reform on adolescents. They found that full-time work for poor mothers was associated with negative effects on adolescents in attitudes toward school, behavioral and emotional problems, criminal activity, use of cigarettes and drugs, and sexual activity. Similarly, Grogger and his coauthors (2002) found that work requirements appeared to impair school performance in adolescent children. Brooks, Hair, and Zaslow (2001) reviewed three experimental studies that showed increased smoking, drinking, and school suspensions, along with reduced school achievement. On the other hand, Chase-Lansdale and coauthors[6] found that a mother's moving

off welfare and into the workforce was associated with improvements in the mental health of her adolescent children.

Overall, then, the great welfare experiment has made little difference
in the well-being of the poor. With the possible exception of adolescents,
who may be negatively affected by the changes, the poor are in the same
boat as before. Sheri Steisel, the director of the human services division
of the National Conference of State Legislatures, summed up the situation when she declared, "There were a lot of people who predicted gloom
and doom, and they were wrong. And there were others who predicted
that we could totally change people's behavior and end poverty, and that
hasn't happened either."[7]

A second conclusion emerges from these studies: *families that are better
off have received increased financial support from the government.* Although
the government has seemingly cut financial support to welfare recipients,
the truth is that many recipients actually get more aid than before. The
difference is that this new assistance is tied to work through an increased
earned income tax credit, day care subsidies, programs to extend Medicaid to children, and other work incentives (Besharov 2003, 17). Since
the 1996 legislation gives states so much flexibility, the financial support
to working mothers varies considerably across the nation. Morris and
her coauthors reviewed five large-scale studies that examine 11 welfare
experiments and concluded that "a comparison of findings for the 11
programs . . . reveals a critical trade-off: Mandatory services [i.e., work
requirements] by themselves have few effects on children and can save
the government money; earning supplements can benefit children, but
they are more costly" (2001, 64). Grogger and his coauthors, after
reviewing 67 studies on the effect of welfare reform, come to similar conclusions: "Work requirements do not appear to have strong impacts on
grade school–age children. . . . Reductions in behavior and school problems are limited to financial work incentives, either implemented alone
or in combination with work requirements, but only for grade school–age
children" (2002, 2). Similarly, Fein and his coauthors find that the only
welfare programs that improved the stability of two-parent families were
the ones that increased income (2002, 5).

The third and final point to take away from these studies is that *there
is little information about welfare reform in a declining economy.* The
National Bureau of Economic Research has determined that the American
economy fell into a recession in March 2001, but the downturn was brief,

lasting only to November 2001. This gives us little information about the effects of welfare changes in hard times. There is clear evidence that the recession increased the demand for emergency services like soup kitchens, food pantries, and homeless shelters,[8] but disentangling the effects of the recession from the effects of welfare reform itself is difficult.

There is some suggestion that attitudes at welfare agencies may have further reduced the welfare rolls by discouraging people hit by the recession from asking for help. The New York City Coalition Against Hunger reports that, from 2000 to 2002, the demand for soup kitchens and food pantries increased by 45 percent and unemployment in New York City increased by 44 percent, but participation in the federal Food Stamps program (which is administered by state welfare agencies) actually *fell* by 4 percent.[9] Similarly, the Center on Budget and Policy Priorities reports that the percentage of poor parents on Medicaid has fallen.[10] While these data do not come from controlled studies, they do suggest that further study is needed to ensure that the new welfare system functions effectively as a safety net for families hit by hard economic times.

Welfare as a Lifeboat

What emerges from a review of the evidence on welfare's effects is a system that is less powerful than critics of either the right or the left contend. Most analysts who have investigated the variety of forces affecting poor people find that welfare is not a major factor in their behavior. And those who have examined the numerous government programs designed to change that behavior have come away with a chastened view of our ability to do so. Government is neither the source of our problems with poverty, nor their cure. At present, the problem of welfare cannot be solved by pushing forward on the lever of government activism (as liberals contend) or by pulling backward to further restrain government (as conservatives assert). The lever of government policy is largely disconnected from the underlying factors affecting the poor. After an in-depth examination of one welfare mother's life in Chicago, Jason DeParle wrote,

> as the details of May Ann Moore's life accrue, welfare itself seems to shrink in importance, compared with the surrounding problems, like low wages, unaffordable rents, gangs, violence, rickety cars, drugs and irresponsible men. . . . Welfare is less a supervillain than a shady character on the corner who accomplishes neither great good nor great ill but invites suspicion by his very presence.[11]

Although his observation is based on a single case study, DeParle's comment neatly summarizes the results of the numerous higher-order empirical studies discussed in this chapter.

In terms of the five-part division of government functions discussed in chapter 1 (redistributional, investment, service, regulatory, and behavioral), welfare, like most programs, is a composite. TANF is, at bottom, a redistributional program, which transfers money to poor people. Medicaid is a service program, bringing health care to people who wouldn't otherwise receive it. The strings and inducements attached to these programs—the requirements for work, the encouragements to reduce out-of-wedlock births, and the child care—are intended to change the behavior of the poor. The empirical literature on welfare suggests that the behavioral component of welfare has little impact, with one big exception—poor people are working more. Their lifestyles are no different, their marriage and birth decisions are unchanged, their education choices are unaffected, and their struggle against poverty is the same, but they are working more. Does this mean that we should dismantle welfare? Should we simply give up on the poor? Not at all. Even though we cannot solve the welfare problem, we are left with the insoluble difficulties of the poor. Although the *economics* of poverty appear to have no ready solution, the *morality* of poverty still haunts us. Even if we can do little to change the underlying fundamentals, we *can* reduce hardship and suffering.

To return to our earlier distinction, even if government programs cannot affect social change, they can serve a humanitarian purpose. According to all the evidence we have, the Food Stamp and WIC supplemental food programs have indeed reduced hunger and malnutrition among the poor, and the Medicaid program has improved their health (Blank 1997, 176–83). As noted above, making the poor better off requires additional public financial support, whether in work incentives or in some other form. Even if welfare reform has not hurt the poor, it has left them in the same miserable straits as before. And it has not relieved us of the moral responsibility to reduce suffering when we have the means to do so.

We have been asking welfare to do more than it can. The sad truth is that, given our current state of knowledge and our current political environment, welfare cannot serve as much of a ladder out of poverty. The hardships of poverty are too fundamental, too deep rooted, to be much affected by short-term government policy. What welfare can do is function as a lifeboat, a safety net, to relieve suffering and hardship. Our faith in the power of government policy has led us to incorrectly push a lot of recipients out of the boat, believing that learning to swim will make them better off. All the evidence suggests that we still need the lifeboat.

Welfare in the "Leverless" State

Our current euphoria over welfare reform is illusory. To see welfare clearly, we have to separate it from the broader economic and social trends with which it is all too frequently confused. Both sides, left and right, have unfairly blamed the welfare system for ills that are actually the result of much broader social changes. Welfare is a whipping boy for our frustrations with rising teenage births, the decline of manufacturing, stagnant real wage rates, and urban decay. We appeal to politicians to pull short-term governmental levers that have little effect on the under-lying problems. Under the belief that these solutions work, that we can easily alter powerful social forces, the new welfare system permits us to treat the poor shabbily. By contrast, when these illusions are stripped away, when we understand the impotence of short-term governmental levers (both those of liberals and those of conservatives), welfare becomes an imperfect response to a powerful set of social forces that are largely beyond our control. This chastened view of welfare's possibilities sug-gests reforms for the welfare system that would be distinctly different from those enacted in 1996.

The fundamental dilemmas of welfare are not economic, but ethical: knowing that government can do little, pro or con, about the funda-mental conditions facing the poor, whom should we help, and under what circumstances? Of course we should continue the experimentation that has provided so much knowledge about welfare's effects. Although previous efforts have not transformed the circumstances of the poor, a new approach could be much more effective. But these demonstration projects should cover truly new ideas and not be retrials of approaches that we know do not work. The "new" welfare system allows many states to follow paths that are known dead ends.

Understanding the powerlessness of government policy may actually bring liberals and conservatives together. Liberals might stop asking for big new programs based on failed old models. And conservatives, under-standing the lack of easy solutions for the poor, might agree to a more humane welfare system. Knowing that two-thirds of the poor are children, and that getting tough with their parents is not likely to help those children much, makes the welfare system more palatable.

Welfare in the leverless state, then, would be more generous than in our current system, because without our illusions we cannot dodge the simple moral requirement to reduce suffering. For the working poor, we might further raise the minimum wage, increase the earned income tax credit, and increase child support, as suggested by David Ellwood (1988). In my view, these changes are not likely to have a large impact on the number of the poor in the workforce, but they are all good ways to channel more income to the poor and relieve the pain that poverty brings. Since our focus should be on increasing income, the form of the assistance isn't crucial as long as it helps broad cross-sections of the poor.

If we understood our limitations in welfare, the demand for time-limited welfare would be reduced, since it is based in large part on an unrealistic understanding of the power of government policy. If the fortunes of poor people are largely independent of government policy, there is less rationale to cut them off after a certain date. The suffering caused by that cutoff is the much the same after two years as it is after one month.

On the other hand, a more realistic welfare program would still demand that all welfare recipients work, because that demand is built on moral rather than economic grounds. But our expectations of that work would change. Welfare recipients would be required to work, not because it necessarily constitutes a "magic bullet" out of poverty, but because it seems a fair exchange for the assistance society has offered them. It strengthens their dignity and ours. Seen in this light, public sector employment, even if it does not lead to something better later on, is acceptable. Since a large segment of the poor do not find jobs, even after leaving welfare, programs of public sector employment may be required, especially during economic downturns. Such programs may not change the circumstances of the poor much and may not even save the government much money, but there is a fundamental ethical rationale for them.

The central point is that we must begin to concentrate on what welfare *can* do instead of what it *cannot* do. We have been obsessed with using welfare to change people's lives, even though the data suggest that welfare cannot do this. We must not allow this obsession to blind us to welfare's demonstrated potential to reduce hardship in an imperfect world.

10

Conclusions
Policy as Patent Medicine

I n the late 19th century, patent medicines enjoyed their heyday. Newspapers and magazines were filled with advertisements for nostrums such as "Dr. Lindley's Epilepsy Remedy," "Mixer's Cancer and Scrofula Syrup," and "Tuberculozyne: The New Remedy for Consumption."[1] Traveling medicine shows toured the countryside and entertained with singers, comedians, and jugglers in addition to their sales pitch. These preparations usually consisted of little more than herbs mixed in alcohol, but Americans used them to treat a huge variety of diseases, including cancer, indigestion, constipation, headache, fatigue, sinusitis, rheumatism, and asthma. Remarkably, single compounds were often touted as curing a wide spectrum of ills: Dr. Morse's Indian Root Pills were said to treat jaundice, dysentery, eczema, kidney disease, colds, headache, malarial fever, and rheumatism, as well as conditions which were colorfully described as "piles, biliousness, gravel, and La Grippe" (Shaw 1972).

Many of these remedies did have theoretical underpinnings in the medical knowledge of ancient times. Greek, Roman, and medieval physicians believed that illness was caused by an imbalance of the "the four humors," black bile, yellow bile, phlegm, and blood. The physician's job, then, was to rebalance these humors by stimulating the humor which opposed the overproduced element. The ancient theory of health is both subtle and complex, involving a classification of treatments by color, season, temperature, moisture content, and universal element (earth, air, fire, or water). In addition to supplying the appropriate counterbalancing agent, doctors could also affect a new equilibrium by bloodletting and purging.[2]

These theories and treatments seem ludicrous now, but people believed in them for two reasons. First, they desperately wanted to find relief from their afflictions. As noted in chapter 1, psychologists have demonstrated that humans engage in an "illusion of control" rather than admit the cold truth when nothing can be done. Second, patients didn't know any better, and they didn't have the tools for sorting out conflicting claims. The germ theory of disease, the scientific method, and the rigorous study of anatomy were all in their infancy.

Some patent medicines were actually harmful because they contained opium, cocaine, or high concentrations of alcohol. But most were harmless mixtures that did little. However, even harmless treatments caused suffering in another sense: they diverted scarce cash from other necessities, such as food, clothing, and housing. And the mistaken belief that these medicines worked might have slowed progress in investigating legitimate treatments.

Today we find ourselves in a 21st century traveling medicine show in policy. We debate the merits of various policies to combat poverty, hunger, homelessness, and unemployment, but we don't pay much attention to whether the treatments actually work. The treatments' supporters have theoretical foundations for their arguments that seem plausible. Conservatives, for example, often argue that our social problems are created by perverse incentives and constraints on individual initiative. Liberals often argue that these problems can be traced back to inadequate education or lack of opportunity.

From these theoretical bases, policymakers then prescribe policy treatments that, like patent medicines, are often believed to treat a huge variety of social ills. Conservatives contend, for example, that cutting welfare benefits will ultimately help poor people by restoring their incentives to work and making them a part of working America. According to conservatives, these cuts would also free the middle class and the rich from stiflingly high taxes, stimulating more work and savings. Further, they would make us more competitive internationally by providing businesses with more cheap labor.

On the liberal side, universal health care is held to reduce medical costs because citizens will get the preventive medicine they need. Liberals have also claimed that universal health care will make businesses more competitive by reducing the cost of health insurance for their employees.

And it would get poor women off the welfare rolls because they would not lose their health insurance if they went to work in low-wage jobs. The range of alleged effects from these social nostrums is striking.

Unfortunately, as demonstrated in this book, the elixirs of both conservatives and liberals often deliver much less then they promise:

1. Sports stadiums do not deliver the economic development "punch" touted by their supporters (chapter 1).
2. Despite the attention paid to the economy, presidents have relatively little control over the short-term fluctuations in unemployment, economic growth, and inflation. And despite widespread suspicions that government deficits cause high interest rates and inflation, the empirical evidence for these effects is unclear at this time (chapter 3).
3. Although particular programs might be helpful, there is little evidence that tax cuts or public investments in education or infrastructure will change the economy's growth (chapter 4).
4. Increased spending on education can probably improve students' academic performance, but the effects are small relative to the effects of socioeconomic and family status. As a result, the playing field for economic opportunity is not level, and the children of the poor face greater obstacles than the children of the rich and middle class (chapter 6).
5. State and local governments probably can stimulate their economies through tax cuts and business incentives, but the resulting increase in economic activity is not enough to replace the lost tax revenue. As a result, economic stimulus can only be "purchased" through higher taxes on other taxpayers or reduced spending on other public services such as education (chapter 7).
6. Welfare reform has dramatically reduced the welfare rolls but has not improved the lives of welfare recipients. Welfare itself is not the cause of poverty and has little effect on birth rates among the poor (chapter 9).

As discussed in chapter 1, although government programs can be successful as redistributional, investment, service, or regulatory activities, they often fail in the behavioral dimension. In general, government's ability to alter the behavior of individuals or firms is more limited than is generally recognized.

Just like patients in the late 19th century, we believe in inflated promises for two reasons. First, we engage in the illusion of control. We desperately want to believe that we can control the pace and direction of our economic system; it is just too frightening to realize that we are at the mercy of external forces like globalization. We desperately want to believe that our education system gives all kids an equal chance to succeed; it is disturbing to admit that the accomplishments of the middle class and the rich are not always the result of innate talent or hard work. We desperately want to believe in some relatively easy way to help the poor, and that if they haven't succeeded it is due to their own lack of initiative; otherwise, we are forced to make painful moral choices about what to share with them.

Second, we believe in oversold promises because we don't have the requisite knowledge to judge policy options or the tools to distinguish high-quality from low-quality data. As demonstrated in chapter 8, undergraduate economics courses provide little information about the magnitude of real-world parameters. Nonmajors, the majority of students, take one or two introductory courses that concentrate on the machinery of demand and supply. Majors take additional core courses that have little empirical content, even in courses on statistics and econometrics. Empirical studies are relegated to some of the field courses, and the knowledge gained is scattershot and uneven.

If the situation is bad in undergraduate economics, it is even worse in law school, the postgraduate training most favored by members of Congress. As we have seen in chapter 8, no more than 3 percent of students in top law schools are given formal statistical training. Law students are trained to think deductively, applying the principles of law to specific, unique cases; they have little experience in the inductive process of estimating empirical quantities from separate pieces of data. As a result, they have little expertise in estimating the likely effects of proposed legislation. As we saw in chapter 5, legislation can get passed with limited empirical evaluation. Compared with the evidence used to make health care decisions, the empirical foundations underlying domestic policy decisions are remarkably weak.

Without experience in sorting out good evidence from bad and without even understanding that policy questions can be empirically tested, policymakers and citizens simply make assumptions about the sizes of relevant parameters. My experience is that people typically make these assumptions based on an ideological perspective or their limited personal experiences. Once made, these assumptions are often difficult to dislodge, even with strong opposing evidence.

Of course, having the appropriate information and analysis doesn't guarantee wise decisions. Politics still matters, and elites may not always pursue the common good. But understanding the evidence is a crucial prerequisite to any effective reform. No matter how sophisticated the political reform proposal, progress can't be made if voters and elites don't see their choices clearly.

Recommendations: A New Curriculum

The discussion in this book, although sobering, is not meant to be fatalistic. Some domestic policies do work, and we must keep experimenting to find more effective programs. We should keep seeking better solutions to the problems of poverty, education, economic development, and macroeconomic policy, because the social payoff would be enormous. However, those policy experiments must be based on a thorough understanding of the previous policy programs and their failures—otherwise, we risk repeating old mistakes.

To see our current policy choices clearly and to design policy experiments that truly expand our knowledge of social problems and feasible solutions, policymakers need a better background in empirical methods. In the discussion below, I recommend changes to high school, undergraduate economics, and law school curricula.

However, to be true to the empirical standards advocated in this book, I must first describe the limitations of these recommendations. I have been unable to find a high school, department of economics, or law school that teaches statistics in the way described below, so I am unable to present comprehensive evidence for my recommendations. Rather, I suggest a modest experiment similar to the first clinical trials of a promising new drug, in which one or two high schools, one or two economics departments, or one or two law schools try this new approach. Then, five years after graduation, I suggest that graduates of the "experimental" and "control" (comparable schools with traditional curricula) programs be surveyed to measure their satisfaction with their education. Did their education prepare them adequately for the realities of their careers? If the experimental schools do better than the control schools in student satisfaction, this would constitute good evidence for more widespread adoption of the new curriculum.

Curriculum Changes in High School

As we saw in chapter 2, although the technical details of evaluation studies are complex, it is relatively easy to teach the pitfalls of different kinds of statistical evidence and explain the hierarchy of statistics. Therefore, I recommend that an expanded version of chapter 2 be added to the curricula in high school math or social studies courses. Such a module would probably require between a week and a month of class time—well worth the effort, given the payoff in understanding real-world claims about both personal and policy choices.

Curriculum Changes in Undergraduate Economics

I recommend three changes to the undergraduate economics curriculum to give students a better understanding of the empirical magnitude of key economic parameters: (1) require concurrent enrollment in economic statistics and introductory economics; (2) inject empirical issues, controversies, and studies into the economics core courses; and (3) make economic statistics more empirical. The key points are to teach the required statistics course earlier in the major, to make the statistics course less theoretical and more applied, and to include more empirical information in the other major courses.

Require Concurrent Enrollment in Economic Statistics and Introductory Economics

Instructors in statistics and social science courses encounter a catch-22: if they teach the social science courses first, the students have no statistical background and so can't do the statistical work that allows them to understand estimates of empirical magnitudes. This forces faculty to give their courses a theoretical orientation, which in turn leads to many of the problems described in this book. On the other hand, if instructors teach the statistics first, the students in the statistics class will know little about the social science discipline, which means instructors have no context in which to provide real-world examples for the statistical tools. Also, since the students don't know the central issues in the field, the study of statistics itself seems theoretical and pointless.

To break this catch-22, I require concurrent enrollment in statistics and the introductory course I teach (Introduction to Public Policy).

This arrangement improves both courses: it allows the instructor to include empirical articles and content in the introductory course, thus preventing it from becoming too theoretical, and it motivates the study of statistics by including examples and articles that directly relate to a subject of interest to the student. Also, this arrangement exposes non-majors to empirical tools they would not otherwise learn, since non-majors don't generally take statistics. If students major in economics, this requirement allows them to take statistics earlier in their college careers. Thus, subsequent courses can use these empirical tools to explore the empirical magnitudes of subfields such as poverty, labor, public finance, or trade.

Some departments may feel that this requirement for concurrent enrollment imposes too great a burden on the nonmajor, consuming excessive class time for a person who just wants to learn some basic principles of economics. In those departments, perhaps it would be possible to link economic statistics with intermediate microeconomics or macroeconomics. This arrangement would yield the same benefits of linking substance and statistics, and by and large it would affect only economics majors. If problems of scheduling or coordination are just too great to teach concurrent classes, I would simply suggest teaching economic statistics as early in the student's major career as possible—perhaps right after the introductory economic course or courses. Requiring statistics before the student takes subsequent courses would allow later instructors to draw on those empirical tools in teaching their courses, adding much-needed empirical content.

Inject Empirical Issues, Controversies, and Studies into the Economics Core Courses

When students have the proper background in statistics, instructors can insert empirical content into the core courses. The following concrete suggestions for the four courses should be considered illustrative and not comprehensive; no doubt other economists will devise numerous other ways to inject empirical content into these courses.

Introductory Microeconomics

- The class can discuss estimates of the elasticity of labor supply for men, women, and teenagers; for different income classes; and for different educational attainment levels. These parameters are crucial for consideration of tax policy, welfare policy, and minimum-wage legislation.

- The class can discuss studies of the effect of welfare on the work effort and fertility of the poor.
- The class can discuss estimates of demand and supply elasticities in markets with price ceilings and floors—for example, housing and agriculture markets. This would help illustrate the size of the shortages and surpluses created by government policies, so that students could better gauge the policies' costs and benefits.
- The class can discuss estimates of demand and supply elasticities in markets with tariffs and quotas. Again, this would help students understand the true costs and benefits of these policies.

Introductory Macroeconomics

- The class can review estimates of the effect of interest rates and tax rates on savings and investment, a vital question in tax policy for capital markets.
- The class can review articles on the effect of savings on national growth, crucial literature for discussions of taxation and monetary policy.
- The class can review the track record on fiscal policy and discuss its effectiveness as a stabilization tool.
- The class can review the literature on the marginal propensity to consume out of income, a crucial variable in calculating the multiplier effect of government spending on the economy.

Intermediate Microeconomics

- The instructor can change the name of the course from Price Theory or Microeconomic Theory to Intermediate Microeconomics to reflect the addition of empirical material.
- The class can include material on economic dynamics—how markets transit from one equilibrium to another.
- The class can include material on the roles of innovation, entrepreneurs, and cultural factors in markets.
- The class can include studies of actual consumer behavior, as opposed to predicted behavior according to theory. In what ways are the theoretical conclusions upheld by the studies, and in what ways do consumers diverge from the theory?

- The class can include studies on "welfare triangles" or "excess burdens." These are graphical representations of the inefficiencies created by government interference in the marketplace. Giving students an understanding of these magnitudes would help them better analyze the trade-offs involved in government policy.
- The class can include studies of the actual market structure in current industries, so that the theories of perfect competition, monopoly, and oligopoly can be evaluated as tools in understanding real market behavior.

Intermediate Macroeconomics

- The instructor can change the name of the course from Macroeconomic Theory to Intermediate Macroeconomics to reflect the addition of empirical material.
- The class can present studies on the actual slopes of the investment/saving (IS), liquidity preference/money supply (LM), aggregate demand, and aggregate supply curves. These are curves on graphs used in theoretical macroeconomics; including the actual slopes would help students appreciate the efficacy of different government policies in stabilizing the economy.
- The instructor can present studies testing the foundations and accuracy of Keynesianism, monetarism, and rational expectations theory. Presenting empirical tests on these three influential theories in contemporary macroeconomics would help students assess the realism of these theories.
- The class can present studies assessing evidence for the crowding-out effect.

Make Economic Statistics More Empirical

Undergraduate economic statistics courses are surprisingly abstract in their content, emphasizing mastery of the theory behind statistical operations rather than real-world magnitudes or empirical investigations. I suggest that these courses trim some of the more theoretical material and replace it with real empirical studies on compelling social issues. Let students apply what they have learned by reading journal articles that incorporate these techniques. Literature reviews and meta-analyses such as those published in the *Journal of Economic Literature* would also be helpful. And students could do original research on topics of their own choosing, as a way of introducing them to the strengths and limitations of empirical research.

Curriculum Changes in Law School

Requiring all law students to take a class in statistics would probably be asking too much. After all, the majority of lawyers are in private practice, not public service, and for them the deductive, incremental methods taught in law school seem to work well. But given the number of lawyers in policymaking positions, every law school should offer an optional statistics course that would cover evidence and procedures used in public policy decisions. This would cover the material in chapter 2, descriptive statistics, and inferential statistics such as linear regression and analysis of variance. Students interested in public service should be encouraged to take the course.[3]

The Cost of Our Illusions

When patients bought patent medicines, they sacrificed whatever goods or services they would have purchased had they known the medicines were ineffective. And they also sacrificed whatever research and effort they could have put into finding real solutions to their medical problems. In short, they lost the opportunity to make better decisions with their money.

Our policy illusions, too, carry costs, although they may be a bit more subtle. When we succumb to these illusions, we lose the opportunity to make better choices with our votes and our public funds. Our belief in the power of government to change the behavior of individuals and firms distracts us from the real choices in redistributional, investment, service, and regulatory activities.

If we elect presidents based on short-term economic factors, when they have little effect on those things, we miss the chance to debate and weigh the real choices before us—designing a fair tax code, organizing an effective military, and ensuring clean water and air, for example. And, once in office, the president's time and attention is focused on "the economy, stupid," rather than on these other issues.

If we elect governors based on their reputations to foster economic development, we miss the chance to discuss what a governor can actually do—provide for public education, assist the poor, and maintain highways, for example. This encourages an elected governor to spend time chasing new plants from multinational firms rather than making sure state agencies work efficiently. If we make welfare policy based on the idea that a change in policy will alter the behavior of the poor, we miss the opportunity to honestly debate what poor people need to survive and how much we as a society can afford to give them. Policymakers' attention becomes focused on what behavioral rules should be imposed on the poor, rather than on what policies—health care, food stamps, child care, and so on—can really alleviate suffering.

Our illusions are not inevitable. Given the right information, and given the right tools to judge policy options, we can look more deeply and choose more wisely. With the right training, we can transform our national debate from a discussion of chimeras and mirages into a more rational debate about the real choices confronting us.

Notes

Chapter 1. Introduction

1. Barack Obama, interview by Anderson Cooper, *Anderson Cooper 360*, CNN, February 3, 2009. http://www.cnn.com/2009/POLITICS/02/03/obama.qanda/index.html.

2. The evidence used in this book relates to domestic policy initiatives in the United States and cannot be used to evaluate the much larger policy differences *between* nations. So, for example, chapter 9 examines the effects of the welfare reform act of 1996, but these data should not be used to make arguments about moving to a social welfare state like those in Scandinavia.

3. Throughout this book, I have been careful to not automatically associate the words "liberal" and "conservative" with the first and second views, because the ideological lines are often confusing. For example, in the case of local economic development, many conservatives, especially local industry leaders, oppose larger "public spending" on things like welfare but nevertheless support public sector initiatives to encourage private sector growth. Many liberals, especially those in social service industries, support a larger public budget but oppose publicly assisted private sector initiatives such as sports stadiums, which they feel primarily benefit the middle and upper classes.

4. Author's calculations, based on examination of the online catalogs of the six schools (see chapter 8).

5. The American National Election Studies are a joint project of Stanford University and the University of Michigan.

6. Author's calculations, based on Sapiro and Rosenstone (2004).

Chapter 2. How to Tell What the Emperor Is Wearing

1. The hierarchy assumes that each technique involves similar information detail. This may not always be the case; for example, a small study of a few welfare recipients may allow researchers to do ethnographic research during which the analyst actually lives with the subjects and gathers extensive information, while researchers in a large survey may only be able to spend half an hour with each participant. In such a case, ranking various kinds of studies becomes more difficult.

2. Coalition for Evidence-Based Policy, no date, http://www.evidencebased programs.org.

Chapter 3. It's Not the Economy, Stupid!

1. James Rosen, "Jobs May Be Focal Point in Ohio Race," *Sacramento Bee*, March 1, 2004, A1.

2. David Finkel, "It's a Victory for People Like Us," *Washington Post*, October 26, 2004, A3.

3. Author's calculations, using data from the official web site of the Federal Reserve Board, http://www.federalreserve.gov/bios/boardmembership.htm.

4. As it turned out, this tax cut did initially hit the target: the checks arrived in households right about the time the 2001 recession began. But this cannot be considered a complete victory for short-run fiscal policy, because the tax cuts were not repealed after the end of the recession.

5. I could not find an answer from one of the interviewees, Christina Romer, in the book. However, her position is clearly stated in her article "What Ended the Great Depression?" (1992).

6. According to Barro (1974), such rational thinking by consumers would even extend beyond the grave. If government debt is repaid after the citizens' deaths, they will still save enough to protect their heirs. Assuming that citizens plan to allocate savings between themselves and their heirs, the government's deficits will disrupt these plans, and wise consumers will increase savings to restore the original allocation.

Chapter 4. Growth Illusions

1. Jude Wanniski, "Sketching the Laffer Curve," *Yorktown Patriot*, June 14, 2005.

2. See President Bush's statements at the signing ceremonies for each bill (2001, http://georgewbush-whitehouse.archives.gov/news/releases/2001/06/20010607.html; 2003, http://georgewbush-whitehouse.archives.gov/news/releases/2003/05/20030528-9.html; and 2005, http://georgewbush-whitehouse.archives.gov/news/releases/2006/05/2006 0517-2.html).

3. Larry Kudlow, "Riding the Right Curve: Laffer Days Are Here Again," *National Review* Online, March 11, 2006, http://www.nationalreview.com/kudlow/kudlow2006 03111211.asp.

4. Congressional Record, House, "The Official Truth Squad," remarks by Congresswoman Thelma Drake, July 25, 2006, H5833.

5. Congressional Record, House, "The Federal Budget Deficit," remarks by Congressman Henry Cuellar, February 16, 2005, H697.

6. All figures in this chapter are author's calculations based on U.S. Office of Management and Budget (2007b).

7. Dynarski and Scott-Clayton (2006) do suggest that other need-based programs have been effective, including the Social Security Student Benefit program (now defunct) and Georgia's HOPE scholarship program.

8. *Treasury Bulletin*, March 2007, table OFS-2.

Chapter 5. A Tale of Two Decisions

1. William Greider, "The Education of David Stockman," *Atlantic Monthly*, December 1981, 27.

2. William Greider, "The Education of David Stockman," *Atlantic Monthly*, December 1981, 38.

3. William Greider, "The Education of David Stockman," *Atlantic Monthly*, December 1981, 44.

4. June Goodfield, "Vaccine on Trial," *Science*, March 1984, 79–84.

5. June Goodfield, "Vaccine on Trial," *Science*, March 1984, 79–84.

6. "Hepatitis Vaccine OK'd," *FDA Consumer*, February 1982, 2. The hepatitis B vaccine had been the subject of some controversy, as schools required the vaccine for all children to enroll in kindergarten. This is quite a different decision, and a different controversy, than was faced by Commissioner Hayes; he was asked to approve the vaccine only for high-risk individuals.

7. By "inferential statistics," I mean procedures for hypothesis testing (distinguishing between random differences in patient outcomes and true treatment effects) or for controlling confounding factors (separating the effects of the factors of interest from the effects of other factors).

8. Interested readers might want to examine the answer given by Shulock (1999).

Chapter 6. Is Education the Great Equalizer?

1. Greenwald, Hedges, and Laine (1996, 376). In reporting the largest policy impact, I have ignored the .2230 standard deviation increase found in post-1970 studies of teacher ability for two reasons: (1) it is based on just one study, and (2) teacher ability includes many factors (such as temperament and personality) that are not under the direct control of school authorities.

2. Walberg and Fowler (1987). I calculated the median standardized regression coefficient using information from tables 1 and 3.

3. Fowler and Walberg (1991). I calculated the median standardized regression coefficient using information from tables 2 and 3.

4. Sutton and Soderstrom (1999, 336). The authors ran separate regressions for both kinds of variables and used a statistic known as R-squared to measure how much of the variance in test scores is explained by each of the two groups of variables. The R-squared for the demographics regressions averaged three times the R-squared for the school policy regressions.

5. Here I use the figures for students *offered a scholarship* rather than for students *enrolled in private schools*. In any large-scale choice program, some students will choose, for various reasons, not to leave their current schools. As Mayer and his coauthors note (2002, 33), the figures for students offered a scholarship are therefore the most accurate gauge of the average effect of a full-scale voucher program.

6. Howell and his coauthors (2000) do not specify the effects of a *voucher offer* in terms of standard deviations, but they do give the effects of *switching to a private school* as .17 standard deviations after one year and .33 standard deviations after two years. They also conclude that the effects of a voucher offer are about one-half the size of the effects of switching to a private school, so the figures given in the text are one-half of .17 and .33.

7. Dana Tofig, " 'Achievement Gap' Serious," *Atlanta Journal-Constitution,* May 15, 2004, 1E.

Chapter 7. The States and Competition for Economic Development

1. Chris Burritt and Jim Yardley, "First Mercedes-Benz Plant in US: Alabama Wins the Big Prize Site—Site Selection Near Vance Now Official," *Atlanta Journal and Constitution,* September 30, 1993, D1; Donald W. Nauss, "Bids by States to Lure Businesses Likely to Escalate Competition: Alabama's Winning of the Mercedes-Benz Plant with a $250 Million Incentive Package Is Decried," *Los Angeles Times,* October 1, 1993, D1.

2. Allen R. Myerson, "O Governor, Won't You Buy Me a Mercedes Plant?" *New York Times,* September 1, 1996, 3-1.

3. Donald W. Nauss, "Bids by States to Lure Businesses Likely to Escalate Competition: Alabama's Winning of the Mercedes-Benz Plant with a $250 Million Incentive Package Is Decried," *Los Angeles Times,* October 1, 1993, D1.

4. Allen R. Myerson, "O Governor, Won't You Buy Me a Mercedes Plant?" *New York Times,* September 1, 1996, 3-1.

5. Morgan Murphy, "Touchdown!" *Forbes,* August 9, 1999, 54–55.

6. Donald W. Nauss, "Bids by States to Lure Businesses Likely to Escalate Competition: Alabama's Winning of the Mercedes-Benz Plant With a $250 Million Incentive Package Is Decried," *Los Angeles Times,* October 1, 1993, D1.

7. Katherine L. Bradbury, Yolanda K. Kodrzycki, and Robert Tannenwald, "The Effects of State and Local Public Policies on Economic Development: An Overview," *New England Economic Review,* March/April 1997, 1.

8. This is the estimated elasticity for interstate or *intermetropolitan* tax differentials. The likely elasticity for *intrametropolitan* differentials—differences in taxes between two suburbs in the same area, for example—is much larger, although there are far fewer studies

to go on. Bartik reviews seven studies of this type and concludes that the average elasticity is around −1.76 (1992, 107). This means that a 10 percent tax cut in a suburb's taxes, if public services are unaffected, would raise business activity by almost 18 percent.

9. David Woodruff and John Templeman, "Why Mercedes Is Alabama Bound," *Business Week*, October 11, 1993, 138–39.

10. Allen R. Myerson, "O Governor, Won't You Buy Me a Mercedes Plant?" *New York Times*, September 1, 1996, 3-1.

Chapter 8. What Did Your Congressman Learn in School?

1. Critics have long complained that the economics profession is too theoretical; some examples include John Cassidy ("The Decline of Economics," *New Yorker*, December 2, 1996, 50–60) and Mark Blaug ("Disturbing Currents in Modern Economics," *Challenge*, May–June 1998, 11–45). For a slightly older but still important contribution to this literature by a group of mainstream economists, see Commission on Graduate Education in Economics (1991). These articles have focused on economic research and graduate education; however, because members of Congress are not generally exposed to these areas, I focus here on undergraduate economics and law school.

2. "The Best Graduate Schools," *US News and World Report*, April 14, 2003, 52–54.

3. These six departments do not represent a random sample, but economics, like most academic disciplines, is extremely hierarchical, with professors and graduates from highly ranked departments having much more influence than their counterparts in lower-ranked departments. Thus, these six departments are likely to influence curricula in other colleges and universities.

4. From "Courses of Instruction: Economics—Description of Economics 1123, Introduction to Econometrics," Harvard University Registrar's Office, 2005. http://www.registrar.fas.harvard.edu/Courses/Economics.html.

5. These schools were selected by examining three prominent published rankings of law schools: the *US News and World Report* ranking ("The Best Graduate Schools: Schools of Law," April 14, 2003, 70–72), Justice Thomas Brennan's quality ranking from his book *Judging the Law Schools* (1996), and the Educational Quality Ranking developed by Brian Leiter of the University of Texas School of Law (2003, http://www.utexas.edu/law/faculty/bleiter/rankings). These six schools were the only ones to appear in the top 10 of all three rankings.

6. The *Digest of Education Statistics* notes that, in the 2005–2006 academic year, just 1.6 percent of undergraduates majored in economics. See U.S. Department of Education, *Digest of Education Statistics*, 2007, tables 261 and 306, http://nces.ed.gov/programs/digest/2007menu_tables.asp.

Chapter 9. Welfare without Illusions

1. Author's calculations, based on U.S. Congress, House Committee on Ways and Means, *2004 Green Book*, table 7-9. The table lists average monthly benefits in 2002 for 48 states and the District of Columbia (Nebraska and Pennsylvania were omitted). These monthly figures average $327.37, yielding a yearly average of $3,928.41.

2. Author's calculations, based on American Association of Community Colleges, 2004, http://www.aacc.nche.edu.

3. Author's calculations, based on U.S. Census Bureau, *Who's Minding the Kids? Child Care Arrangements: Spring 2005,* table C2, http://www.census.gov/population/www/socdemo/childcare.html. Average weekly expenditures for child care among families below the federal poverty level are $90. With two weeks of vacation, yearly child care costs average $4,500.

4. Cynthia M. Fagnoni, Director of Education, Workforce, and Income Security Issues, testimony before the Subcommittee on Human Resources, House Committee on Ways and Means. GAO/T-HEHS-99-116, May 27, 1999. http://www.gao.gov/archive/1999/he99116t.pdf.

5. P. Lindsay Chase-Lansdale, Robert A. Moffitt, Brenda J. Lohman, Andrew J. Cherlin, Rebekah Levine Coley, Laura D. Pittman, Jennifer Roff, and Elizabeth Votruba-Drzal, "Mothers' Transition from Welfare to Work and the Well-Being of Preschoolers and Adolescents," *Science,* March 2003, 1548–52.

6. P. Lindsay Chase-Lansdale, Robert A. Moffitt, Brenda J. Lohman, Andrew J. Cherlin, Rebekah Levine Coley, Laura D. Pittman, Jennifer Roff, and Elizabeth Votruba-Drzal, "Mothers' Transition from Welfare to Work and the Well-Being of Preschoolers and Adolescents," *Science,* March 2003, 1548–52.

7. Linda Jacobson, "Experts Debate Welfare Reform's Impact on Children," *Education Week* 21(3): 1–8.

8. See, for example, Stephanie Simon, "Homeless Shelters, Charities Swamped as Evictions Soar," *Chicago Tribune,* February 17, 2002.

9. New York City Coalition Against Hunger, "'Hidden Victims' of 9/11 Turned Away from Feeding Programs: Annual Report Details Increasing Food and Resource Gap at Agencies," press release, November 26, 2002.

10. Alexandra Starr, "Is the Economy's Safety Net Recession-Ready?" *Business Week,* June 11, 2001, 132.

11. Jason DeParle, "Better Work Than Welfare: But What If There's Neither?" *New York Times Magazine,* December 18, 1994, 44–74.

Chapter 10. Conclusions

1. Center for Drug Evaluation and Research, U.S. Food and Drug Administration, 2005, "Gallery of Nostrums," http://www.fda.gov/cder/about/history/Gallery/gallery1.htm.

2. N. S. Gill, 2005, "Hippocratic Method and the Four Humors in Medicine," http://ancienthistory.about.com/cs/hippocrates/a/hippocraticmeds.htm.

3. For additional recommendations on improving empirical training in law school, please see Epstein and King (2002).

References

Alloy, L. B., and C. M. Clements. 1992. "Illusion of Control: Invulnerability to Negative Affect and Depressive Symptoms after Laboratory and Natural Stressors." *Journal of Abnormal Psychology* 101(2): 234–45.

Amrein, Audrey L., and David C. Berliner. 2002a. "An Analysis of Some Unintended and Negative Consequences of High-Stakes Testing," working paper, Education Policy Research Unit, College of Education, Arizona State University, December.

———. 2002b. "The Impact of High-Stakes Tests on Student Academic Performance: An Analysis of NAEP Results in States with High-Stakes Tests and ACT, SAT, and AP Test Results in States with High School Graduation Exams," working paper, Education Policy Research Unit, College of Education, Arizona State University, December.

Anderson, John E., and Robert W. Wassmer. 2000. *Bidding for Business: The Efficacy of Local Economic Development Incentives in a Metropolitan Area.* Kalamazoo, MI: W. E. Upjohn Institute for Employment Research.

Barro, Robert. 1974. "Are Government Bonds Net Worth?" *Journal of Political Economy* 82(6): 1095–1117.

Bartik, Timothy J. 1991. *Who Benefits from State and Local Economic Development Policies?* Kalamazoo, MI: W. E. Upjohn Institute for Employment Research.

———. 1992. "The Effects of State and Local Taxes on Economic Development: A Review of Recent Research." *Economic Development Quarterly* 6(1): 102–11.

———. 1993. "Who Benefits from Local Job Growth: Migrants or the Original Residents?" *Regional Studies* 27(4): 297–331.

———. 1994. "Jobs, Productivity, and Local Economic Development: What Implications Does Economic Research Have for the Role of Government?" *National Tax Journal* 47(4): 847–61.

———. 1996. "Strategies for Economic Development." In *Management Policies in Local Government Finance,* 4th ed., edited by J. Richard Aronson and Eli Schwartz

(287–312). Washington, DC: International City/County Management Association Presses.

Besharov, Douglas. 2003. "The Past and Future of Welfare Reform." *Public Interest* 150: 4–21, Winter.

Blanchard, Olivier Jean, and Lawrence F. Katz. 1992. "Regional Evolutions." *Brookings Papers on Economic Activity* 1: 1–75.

Blank, Rebecca M. 1997. *It Takes a Nation: A New Agenda for Fighting Poverty.* New York: Russell Sage Foundation.

———. 2002. "Evaluating Welfare Reform in the United States." *Journal of Economic Literature* 40(4): 1127–35.

Boller, Paul F. 1981. *Presidential Anecdotes.* New York: Oxford University Press.

Borman, Geoffrey D., and Jerome V. D'Agostino. 1996. "Title I and Student Achievement: A Meta-Analysis of Federal Evaluation Results." *Educational Evaluation and Policy Analysis* 18(4): 309–26.

Brennan, Thomas E. 1996. *Judging the Law Schools.* East Lansing, MI: TEBCO Inc.

Brooks, Jennifer L., Elizabeth C. Hair, and Martha J. Zaslow. 2001. "Welfare Reform's Impact on Adolescents: Early Warning Signs." Child Trends Research Brief, July. http://www.childtrends.org.

Brown, E. Cary. 1956. "Fiscal Policy in the 'Thirties: A Reappraisal." *American Economic Review* 46(5): 857–79.

Buchanan, James M., and Richard E. Wagner. 1977. *Democracy in Deficit: The Political Legacy of Lord Keynes.* London: Academic Press.

Cannon, Lou. 1982. *Reagan.* New York: Putnam Publishers.

Cardiel, Mario H., and Charles H. Goldsmith. 1995. "Type of Statistical Techniques in Rheumatology and Internal Medicine Journals." *Review of Clinical Investigations* 47(3): 197–201.

Carnoy, Martin, Susanna Loeb, and Tiffany L. Smith. 2001. *Do Higher State Test Scores in Texas Make for Better High School Outcomes?* CPRE Research Report Series RR-047. Philadelphia: Center for Policy Research in Education, University of Pennsylvania, Graduate School of Education.

Center on Education Policy. 2002. *State High School Exit Exams: A Baseline Report.* Washington, DC: Center on Education Policy.

———. 2003. *State High School Exit Exams Put to the Test.* Washington, DC: Center on Education Policy.

Chubb, John E., and Terry M. Moe. 1990. *Politics, Markets, and America's Schools.* Washington, DC: Brookings Institution Press.

Commission on Graduate Education in Economics. 1991. "The Report of the Commission on Graduate Education in Economics." *Journal of Economic Literature* 29(3): 1035–87.

Congressional Quarterly. 2002. *CQ's Politics in America 2002: The 107th Congress.* Washington, DC: Congressional Quarterly.

Council of Economic Advisers. 1997. *Explaining the Decline in Welfare Receipt, 1993–1996: Technical Report.* Washington, DC: U.S. Government Printing Office.

————. 1999. *The Effect of Welfare Policy and Economic Expansion on Welfare Caseloads: An Update.* Washington, DC: U.S. Government Printing Office.

Council of State Governments. 2000. *State Business Incentives: Trends and Options for the Future,* 2nd ed. Lexington, KY: Council of State Governments.

————. 2005. *The Book of the States,* vol. 37. Lexington, KY: Council of State Governments.

Courant, Paul N. 1994. "How Would You Know a Good Economic Development Policy If You Tripped Over One? Hint: Don't Just Count Jobs." *National Tax Journal* 47(4): 863–81.

Danziger, Sheldon, Colleen M. Heflin, Mary E. Corcoran, Elizabeth Oltmans, and Hui-Chen Wang. 2002. "Does It Pay to Move from Welfare to Work?" *Journal of Policy Analysis and Management* 21(4): 671–92.

Darrat, Ali F. 1990. "Structural Federal Deficits and Interest Rates: Some Causality and Co-Integration Tests." *Southern Economic Journal* 56(3): 752–59.

Davidson, Roger H. 1976. "Congressional Committees: The Toughest Customers." *Policy Analysis* 2(2): 299–323.

DeLong, J. Bradford. 1996. "Keynesianism, Pennsylvania Avenue Style: Some Economic Consequences of the Employment Act of 1946." *Journal of Economic Perspectives* 10(3): 41–53.

DeLong, J. Bradford, and Lawrence H. Summers. 1986. "The Changing Cyclical Variability of Economic Activity in the United States." In *The American Business Cycle: Continuity and Change,* edited by Robert J. Gordon (679–734). Chicago: University of Chicago Press.

Dusansky, Richard, and Clayton J. Vernon. 1998. "Rankings of U.S. Economics Departments." *Journal of Economic Perspectives* 12(1): 157–70.

Dynarski, Susan M., and Judith E. Scott-Clayton. 2006. "The Cost of Complexity in Federal Student Aid: Lessons from Optimal Tax Theory and Behavioral Economics." *National Tax Journal* 59(2): 319–56.

Edin, Kathryn, and Laura Lein. 1997. *Making Ends Meet: How Single Mothers Survive Welfare and Low Wage Work.* New York: Russell Sage Foundation.

Eisinger, Peter. 1995. "State Economic Development in the 1990s: Politics and Policy Learning." *Economic Development Quarterly* 9(2): 146–58.

Ellwood, David. 1988. *Poor Support.* New York: Basic Books.

Elmendorf, Douglas W., and N. Gregory Mankiw. 1998. "Government Debt." Working Paper 6470. Cambridge, MA: National Bureau of Economic Research.

Emerson, J. D., and G. A. Colditz. 1983. "Use of Statistical Analysis in the *New England Journal of Medicine.*" *New England Journal of Medicine* 309(12): 709–13.

Engen, Eric, and Jonathan Skinner. 1996. "Taxation and Economic Growth." *National Tax Journal* 49(4): 617–42.

Epstein, Lee, and Gary King. 2002. "The Rules of Inference." *University of Chicago Law Review* 69(1): 1–133.

Evans, Paul. 1985. "Do Large Deficits Produce High Interest Rates?" *American Economic Review* 74(1): 68–87.

————. 1986. "Is the Dollar High Because of Large Budget Deficits?" *Journal of Monetary Economics* 18(3): 227–49.

————. 1987. "Do Budget Deficits Raise Nominal Interest Rates? Evidence from Six Countries." *Journal of Monetary Economics* 20(2): 281–300.

————. 1988. "Are Consumers Ricardian? Evidence for the United States." *Journal of Political Economy* 96(5): 983–1004.

Fair, Ray C. 1996. "The Effect of Economic Events on Votes for President: 1992 Update." *Political Behavior* 18(2): 119–39.

Fein, David J., Laura Duberstein Lindberg, Rebecca A. London, and Jane Mauldon. 2002. "Welfare Reform and Family Formation: Assessing the Effects." Abt Associates Research Brief 1, Welfare Reform and Family Formation Project. Bethesda, MD: Abt Associates.

Fisher, Peter S., and Alan H. Peters. 1998. *Industrial Incentives: Competition among American States and Cities.* Kalamazoo, MI: W. E. Upjohn Institute for Employment Research.

Fisher, Ronald C. 1997. "The Effects of State and Local Public Services on Economic Development." *New England Economic Review* March/April: 53–67.

Fowler, William J., and Herbert J. Walberg. 1991. "School Size, Characteristics, and Outcomes." *Educational Evaluation and Policy Analysis* 13(2): 189–202.

Frye, Alton. 1976. "Congressional Politics and Policy Analysis: Bridging the Gap." *Policy Analysis* 2(2): 265–82.

Gale, William G., and Peter R. Orszag. 2005. "Economic Effects of Making the 2001 and 2003 Tax Cuts Permanent." *International Tax and Public Finance* 12(2): 193–232.

Garfinkle, Norton. 2005. "Supply-Side vs. Demand-Side Tax Cuts and Economic Growth." *Critical Review* 17(3 and 4): 427–48.

Gill, Brian P., Mike Timpane, Karen E. Ross, Dominic J. Brewer, and Kevin Booker. 2001. *Rhetoric versus Reality: What We Know and What We Need to Know about Vouchers and Charter Schools.* Santa Monica, CA: RAND.

Goldberger, Marvin, Brendan A. Maher, and Pamela E. Flattau, eds. 1995. *Research-Doctorate Programs in the United States: Continuity and Change.* Washington, DC: National Academy Press.

Gordon, Nora. 2004. "Do Federal Grants Boost School Spending? Evidence from Title I." *Journal of Public Economics* 88(9 and 10): 1771–92.

Gramlich, Edward. 1994. "Infrastructure Investment: A Review Essay." *Journal of Economic Literature* 32(3): 1176–96.

Greenberg, David, Marvin Mandell, and Matthew Onstott. 2000. "The Dissemination and Utilization of Welfare-to-Work Experiments in State Policymaking." *Journal of Policy Analysis and Management* 19(3): 367–82.

Greene, Jay P., William G. Howell, and Paul E. Peterson. 1998. "Lessons from the Cleveland Scholarship Program." In *Learning from School Choice,* edited by Paul E. Peterson and Bryan C. Hassel (357–94). Washington, DC: Brookings Institution Press.

Greene, Jay P., Paul E. Peterson, and Jiangtao Du. 1998. "School Choice in Milwaukee: A Randomized Experiment." In *Learning from School Choice,* edited by Paul E. Peterson and Bryan C. Hassel (335–56). Washington, DC: Brookings Institution Press.

Greenwald, Rob, Larry V. Hedges, and Richard D. Laine. 1996. "The Effect of School Resources on Student Achievement." *Review of Educational Research* 66(3): 361–96.

Grogger, Jeffrey, Lynn A. Karoly, and Jacob A. Klerman. 2002. "Consequences of Welfare Reform: A Research Synthesis." RAND Corporation Report DRU-2676-DHHS. Santa Monica, CA: RAND.

Haney, Walt. 2000. "The Myth of the Texas Miracle in Education." *Education Policy Analysis* 8(41). http://epaa.asu.edu/epaa/v8n41.

Hanushek, Eric. 1997. "Assessing the Effects of School Resources on Student Performance: An Update." *Educational Evaluation and Policy Analysis* 19(2): 141–64.

Hoelscher, Gregory P. 1983. "Federal Borrowing and Short-Term Interest Rates." *Southern Economic Journal* 50(2): 319–33.

Hoover, Kevin D., and Steven M. Sheffrin. 1992. "Causation, Spending, and Taxes: Sand in the Sandbox or Tax Collector for the Welfare State?" *American Economic Review* 82(1): 225–48.

Howell, William G., Patrick J. Wolf, Paul E. Peterson, and David E. Campbell. 2000. "Test Score Effects of School Vouchers in Dayton, Ohio, New York City, and Washington, D.C.: Evidence from Randomized Trials." Paper presented at the American Political Science Association annual meetings, August. Cambridge, MA: Program on Education Policy and Governance, Harvard University.

Hoxby, Caroline M. 2000. "Does Competition among Public Schools Benefit Students and Taxpayers?" *American Economic Review* 90(5): 1209–38.

———. 2001. "If Families Matter Most, Where Do Schools Come In?" In *A Primer on America's Schools*, edited by Terry M. Moe (89–125). Stanford, CA: Hoover Institution Press.

Jacob, Brian A. 2001. "Getting Tough? The Impact of High School Graduation Exams." *Educational Evaluation and Policy Analysis* 23(2): 99–121.

Jamieson, Kathleen Hall. 1992. *Dirty Politics: Deception, Distraction, and Democracy.* New York: Oxford University Press.

Jepsen, Christopher. 2002. "The Role of Aggregation in Estimating the Effects of Private School Competition on Student Achievement." *Journal of Urban Economics* 52(3): 477–500.

Johnston, Louis D., and Samuel H. Williamson. 2005. "The Annual Real and Nominal GDP for the United States, 1790–Present." Economic History Services, October. http://www.eh.net/hmit/gdp/.

Jones, Charles O. 1976. "Why Congress Can't Do Policy Analysis (or Words to That Effect)." *Policy Analysis* 2(2): 251–64.

Juzych, Mark S., Dong H. Shin, Mahmoud Seyedsadr, Scott W. Siegner, and Lydia A. Juzych. 1992. "Statistical Techniques in Ophthalmic Journals." *Archives of Ophthalmology* 110(9): 1225–29.

Kaestner, Robert, Sanders Korenman, and June O'Neill. 2003. "Has Welfare Reform Changed Teenage Behaviors?" *Journal of Policy Analysis and Management* 22(2): 225–48.

Kahlenberg, Richard D. 2001. "Learning from James Coleman." *Public Interest* 144: 54–72, Summer.

Keech, William R. 1995. *Economic Politics: The Costs of Democracy.* New York: Cambridge University Press.

Kirp, David L. 1992. "The End of Policy Analysis: With Apologies to Daniel (*The End of Ideology*) Bell and Francis ("The End of History") Fukiyama." *Journal of Policy Analysis and Management* 11(4): 693–96.

Laffer, Arthur B. 2004. "The Laffer Curve: Past, Present, and Future." Heritage Foundation Backgrounder 1765. http://www.heritage.org/research/taxes/bg1765.cfm.

Langer, Ellen J. 1975. "The Illusion of Control." *Journal of Personality and Social Psychology* 32(2): 311–28.

Lerner, Abba. 1951. *Economics of Employment.* New York: McGraw-Hill.

Levin, Henry M., and Clive R. Belfield. 2002. "Families as Contractual Partners in Education." *UCLA Law Review* 49(6): 1800–24.

Lewis-Beck, Michael S., and Mary Stegmaier. 2007. "Economic Models of Voting." In *The Oxford Handbook of Political Behavior,* edited by Russell Dalton and Hans-Dieter Klingemann (518–37). Oxford, UK: Oxford University Press.

Lindert, Peter H. 2004. *Growing Public: Social Spending and Economic Growth since the Eighteenth Century.* Cambridge: Cambridge University Press.

Lipford, Jody. 1999. "Twenty Years after Humphrey-Hawkins." *Independent Review* 4(1): 41–62.

Martin, Bernard H. 2004. "The Coalition for Evidence-Based Policy: Its Impact on Policy and Practice." Report to the William T. Grant Foundation, New York. http://www.excelgov.org/admin/FormManager/filesuploading/indep_evaln_for_WT_Grant.pdf.

Martin, Joyce A., Brady E. Hamilton, Paul D. Sutton, Stephanie J. Ventura, Fay Menacker, Sharon Kirmeyer, and Martha L. Munson. 2007. "Births: Final Data for 2005." National Vital Statistics Reports 56(6). Hyattsville, MD: National Center for Health Statistics, Centers for Disease Control and Prevention, U.S. Department of Health and Human Services.

Mayer, Bruce D., and James X. Sullivan. 2001. "The Effects of Welfare and Tax Reform: The Material Well-Being of Single Mothers in the 1980s and 1990s." NBER Working Paper 8298. Cambridge, MA: National Bureau of Economic Research.

Mayer, Daniel P., Paul E. Peterson, David E. Myers, Christina Clark Tuttle, and William G. Howell. 2002. *School Choice in New York City after Three Years: An Evaluation of the School Choice Scholarships Program: Final Report.* Cambridge, MA: Harvard University and Mathematica Policy Research.

McGuire, Therese. 1992. "Review of *Who Benefits from State and Local Economic Development Policies?* by Timothy Bartik." *National Tax Journal* 45(4): 457–59.

McMillan, Robert. 2001. "Competition, Parental Involvement, and Public School Performance." *National Tax Association Proceedings: Ninety-Third Annual Conference on Taxation, Santa Fe, New Mexico, November 9–11, 2000,* 150–55.

Metcalf, Kim K., William J. Boone, Frances K. Stage, Todd L. Chilton, Patty Muller, and Polly Tait. 1998. "A Comparative Evaluation of the Cleveland Scholarship and Tutoring Grant Program." Bloomington, IN: Indiana Center for Evaluation, Indiana University.

Moffitt, Robert. 1992. "Incentive Effects of the U.S. Welfare System: A Review." *Journal of Economic Literature* 30(1): 1–61.

Mooney, Christopher Z. 1991. "Information Sources in State Legislative Decision Making." *Legislative Studies Quarterly* 16(3): 445–55.

Morris, Pamela A., Aletha C. Huston, Greg J. Duncan, Danielle A. Crosby, and Johannes M. Bos. 2001. "How Welfare and Work Policies Affect Children: A Synthesis of Research." Report, March. New York: Manpower Demonstration Research Corporation. http://www.mdrc.org/Reports2001/NGChildSynth/NG-ChildSynth.pdf.

Motely, Brian. 1983. "Real Interest Rates, Money, and Government Deficits." *Federal Reserve Bank of San Francisco Economic Review* Summer: 31–45.

Murray, Charles. 1984. *Losing Ground.* New York: Basic Books.

National Bureau of Economic Research. 2008. "Business Cycle Expansions and Contractions." Cambridge, MA: Public Information Office, National Bureau of Economic Research. http://www.nber.org/cycles.html.

National Center for Education Statistics. 2003. *School District Expenditures for Elementary and Secondary Education: 1997–98.* Statistical Analysis Report. Washington, DC: U.S. Department of Education.

National Research Council, Advisory Committee on Government Programs in the Behavioral Sciences. 1968. *The Behavioral Sciences and the Federal Government.* Washington, DC: National Research Council.

Nelson, Carnot E., Jeanne Roberts, Cynthia M. Maedcrer, Bruce Wertheimer, and Beverly Johnson. 1987. "The Utilization of Social Science Information by Policymakers." *American Behavioral Scientist* 30(6): 569–77.

Noll, Roger G., and Andrew Zimbalist. 1997. *Sports, Jobs, and Taxes: The Economic Impact of Sports Teams and Stadiums.* Washington, DC: Brookings Institution Press.

Nutley, Sandra M., H. T. O. Davies, and Peter C. Smith. 2000. *What Works: Evidence-Based Policy and Practice in Public Services.* Bristol, UK: Policy Press.

Parker, Randall E. 2007. *The Economics of the Great Depression: A Twenty-First Century Look Back at the Economics of the Interwar Era.* Cheltenham, UK. Edward Elgar Publishing.

Peppers, Larry C. 1973. "Full Employment Surplus Analysis and Structural Change: The 1930s." *Explorations in Economic History* 10(2): 197–210.

Phillips, Joseph M., and Ernest Goss, 1995. "The Effect of State and Local Taxes on Economic Development: A Meta-Analysis." *Southern Economic Journal* 62(2): 320–33.

Plosser, Charles I. 1982. "Government Financing Decisions and Asset Returns." *Journal of Monetary Economics* 9(3): 325–52.

———. 1987. "Fiscal Policy and the Term Structure." *Journal of Monetary Economics* 20(2): 343–67.

Portney, Paul R. 1976. "Congressional Delays in U.S. Fiscal Policymaking: Simulating the Effects." *Journal of Public Economics* 5(3–4): 237–47.

Puma, Michael J., Nancy Karweit, Cristofer Price, Anne Ricciuti, William Thompson, and Michael Vaden-Kiernan. 1997. *Prospects: The Congressionally Mandated Study of Educational Growth and Opportunity—Final Report.* Washington, DC: U.S. Department of Education.

Rappaport, Jordan, and Chad Wilkerson. 2001. "What Are the Benefits of Hosting a Major League Sports Franchise?" *Federal Reserve Bank of Kansas City Economic Review* 86: 55–86, 1st quarter.

Raynold, Prosper, W. Douglas McMillin, and Thomas R. Beard. 1991. "The Impact of Federal Government Expenditures in the 1930s." *Southern Economic Journal* 58(1): 15–28.

Reznick, Richard K., Elizabeth Dawson-Saunders, and J. Roland Folse. 1987. "A Rationale for the Teaching of Statistics to Surgical Residents." *Surgery* 101(5): 611–17.

Ricciuti, Roberto. 2003. "Assessing Ricardian Equivalence." *Journal of Economic Surveys* 17(1): 55–78.

Romer, Christina. 1992. "What Ended the Great Depression?" *Journal of Economic History* 52(4): 757–84.

Rosenfeld, Richard M., and Howard E. Rockette. 1991. "Biostatistics in Otolaryngology Journals." *Archives of Otolaryngology—Head and Neck Surgery* 117(10): 1172–76.

Sapiro, Virginia, and Stephen J. Rosenstone. 2004. *American National Election Studies Cumulative Data File, 1948–2002.* Ann Arbor, MI: Inter-University Consortium for Political and Social Research.

Shaw, Robert B. 1972. *History of the Comstock Patent Medicine Business and Dr. Morse's Indian Root Pills.* Smithsonian Studies in History and Technology 22. Washington, DC: Smithsonian Institution. (Project Gutenberg, 2005, http://www.gutenberg.org/dirs/1/3/3/9/13397/13397-h/13397-h.htm.)

Shioji, Etsuro. 2001. "Public Capital and Economic Growth: A Convergence Approach." *Journal of Economic Growth* 6(3): 205–27.

Shulock, Nancy. 1999. "The Paradox of Policy Analysis: If It Is Not Used, Why Do We Produce So Much of It?" *Journal of Policy Analysis and Management* 18(2): 226–44.

Siegfried, John J. 2000. "How Many College Students Are Exposed to Economics?" *Journal of Economic Education* 31(2): 202–4.

Sloan, John W. 1999. *The Reagan Effect: Economics and Presidential Leadership.* Lawrence: University Press of Kansas.

Sutton, Alice, and Irina Soderstrom. 1999. "Predicting Elementary and Secondary School Achievement with School-Related and Demographic Factors." *Journal of Educational Research* 92(6): 330–38.

Temple, Jonathan. 1999. "The New Growth Evidence." *Journal of Economic Literature* 37(1): 112–56.

Trzcinski, Eileen, and Jerry Brandell. 2001. "Adolescent Outcomes, Poverty Status, and Welfare Reform: An Analysis Based on the Survey of Program Dynamics." Final report prepared for the Research Development Grant, 2000–2001, U.S. Bureau of the Census, U.S. Department of Health and Human Services, and Joint Center for Poverty Research. Evanston, IL, and Chicago, IL: Joint Center for Poverty Research.

U.S. Bureau of Economic Analysis. 2007. "Current Dollar and 'Real' Gross Domestic Product." http://www.bea.gov/national/xls/gdplev.xls.

U.S. Census Bureau. 1999. *Statistical Abstract of the United States.* Washington, DC: U.S. Government Printing Office.

————. 2004. *Statistical Abstract of the United States.* Washington, DC: U.S. Government Printing Office.

U.S. Office of Education, Department of Health, Education, and Welfare. 1966. *Equality of Educational Opportunity.* Washington, DC: U.S. Government Printing Office. *(Note:* commonly called the Coleman Report.)

U.S. Office of Management and Budget. 2007a. *Analytical Perspectives: Budget of the United States Government, Fiscal Year 2008.* Washington, DC: U.S. Government Printing Office.

————. 2007b. *Budget of the United States Government, Fiscal Year 2008.* Washington, DC: U.S. Government Printing Office.

————. 2008. *Budget of the United States Government, Fiscal Year 2009.* Washington, DC: U.S. Government Printing Office.

Walberg, Herbert J., and William J. Fowler. 1987. "Expenditure and Size Efficiencies of Public School Districts." *Educational Researcher* 16(7): 5–13.

Wasylenko, Michael. 1997. "Taxation and Economic Development: The State of the Economic Literature." *New England Economic Review* March/April: 37–52.

Weiss, Carol H. 1989. "Congressional Committees as Users of Analysis." *Journal of Policy Analysis and Management* 8(3): 411–31.

Weiss, Scott T., and Jonathan M. Samet. 1980. "An Assessment of Physician Knowledge of Epidemiology and Biostatistics." *Journal of Medical Education* 55(8): 692–97.

Whiteman, David. 1995. *Communication in Congress: Members, Staff, and the Search for Information.* Lawrence: University Press of Kansas.

Witte, John. 1998. "The Milwaukee Voucher Experiment." *Educational Evaluation and Policy Analysis* 20(4): 229–51.

About the Author

Paul Gary Wyckoff directs the public policy program at Hamilton College. He teaches courses in applied statistics, ethics, and cost-benefit analysis, as well as issue-oriented courses on topics such as health care reform, education policy, and Social Security reform. Professor Wyckoff studied economics and political science at Hamilton College and later received a Ph.D. in economics from the University of Michigan. Prior to Hamilton, he held positions at the Federal Reserve and Indiana University. Professor Wyckoff has published in numerous journals, including the *Journal of Policy Analysis and Management,* the *Review of Economics and Statistics,* the *Journal of Urban Economics,* and the *Journal of Education Finance.* This is his first book.

Index

DATE DUE
